Principles and Standards for School Mathematics Navigations Series

Navigating

through

Problem Solving

and

Reasoning

in

Grade 5

Denisse R. Thompson
Michael Battista
Sally Mayberry
Karol L. Yeatts
Judith S. Zawojewski

Bonnie H. Litwiller
Grades 3–6 Editor

Peggy A. House
Navigations Series Editor

NATIONAL COUNCIL OF
TEACHERS OF MATHEMATICS

Copyright © 2007 by
The National Council of Teachers of Mathematics, Inc.
1906 Association Drive, Reston, VA 20191-1502
(703) 620-9840; (800) 235-7566; www.nctm.org

Library of Congress Cataloging-in-Publication Data

Navigating through problem solving and reasoning in grade 5 / Denisse R.
Thompson ... [et al.].
    p. cm. -- (Principles and standards for school mathematics
navigations series)
  Includes bibliographical references and index.
  ISBN-13: 978-0-87353-592-2 (alk. paper)
  ISBN-10: 0-87353-592-8 (alk. paper)
  1. Mathematics--Study and teaching (Elementary)--Activity programs. 2. Fifth grade
(Education)--Activity programs. 3. Problem solving in children. 4. Reasoning in
children. I. Thompson, Denisse Rubilee, 1954-
  QA135.6.N374 2007
  372.7'049--dc22
                                                            2006100871

The National Council of Teachers of Mathematics is a public voice of mathematics
education, providing vision, leadership, and professional development to support
teachers in ensuring mathematics learning of the highest quality for all students.

Printed in the United States of America

NAVIGATIONS SERIES

TABLE OF CONTENTS

Contents of the CD-ROM

Introduction

Table of Standards and Expectations, Process Standards, Pre-K–Grade 12

Applet

3-D Shape Decomposition Tool

Blackline Masters and Templates

(All of those listed above, plus the following)

Half-Inch Grid Paper

Quarter-Inch Grid Paper

Four Years of Snow

Excel Spreadsheet of "Four Years of Snow"

Discussions of Work by Students on "Which Month to Ski"

Group 1—Letter

Group 1—Analysis of Data

Group 2—Letter

Group 2—Example

Group 2—Analysis of Data

Group 3—Letter

Group 3—Example A

Group 3—Example B

Readings and Supplemental Materials

Divisibility Tests: So Right for Discoveries
Albert B. Bennett, Jr., and L. Ted Nelson
Mathematics Teaching in the Middle School

A Modeling Perspective on Students' Mathematical Reasoning about Data
Helen M. Doerr and Lyn D. English
Journal for Research in Mathematics Education

Strategies for Advancing Children's Mathematical Thinking
Judith Fraivillig
Teaching Children Mathematics

Students Use Their Bodies to Measure Animals
Eunice Hendrix-Martin
Teaching Children Mathematics

Mathematical Tasks and Student Cognition: Classroom-Based Factors That Support and Inhibit High-Level Mathematical Thinking and Reasoning
Marjorie Henningsen and Mary Kay Stein
Journal for Research in Mathematics Education

About This Book

Navigating through Problem Solving and Reasoning in Grade 5 is the sixth of seven grade-level books that present investigations designed to develop students' reasoning methods and problem-solving strategies. The introduction to the book provides an overview of reasoning and problem solving as they might appear in grade 5 as well as a discussion of the role of the teacher in nurturing the development of students' reasoning and problem-solving abilities. Five explorations follow, each situated in a different one of the five content strands identified in *Principles and Standards for School Mathematics* (National Council of Teachers of Mathematics [NCTM] 2000)—number and operations, algebra, geometry, measurement, and data analysis and probability. For the convenience of the teacher, the Standards and expectations for the Process Standards (which include Problem Solving as well as Reasoning and Proof) appear on the inside front cover of the book.

All the explorations are organized in the same way:

- Focus
- Overview
- Goals
- Mathematical Content
- Prior Knowledge or Experience
- Materials
- Classroom Environment
- Investigation
- Assessment
- Reflections
- Connections

Three different icons appear in this book, as shown in the key. One alerts readers to material quoted from *Principles and Standards for School Mathematics*, another points them to supplementary materials on the CD-ROM that accompanies the book, and a third signals the blackline masters and indicates their locations in the appendix.

All the investigations have blackline masters, which are signaled in the text by an icon. These activity pages are identified in the materials lists for the explorations and appear—along with solutions for the problems—in the appendix. You can also print the blackline pages from the accompanying CD-ROM. Another icon signals content on the CD, which also provides an applet for your students to manipulate as well as resources for your professional development.

Margin notes offer suggestions to aid you in preparing to use the investigations in your classroom. As your students work, take note of the appropriateness of their mathematical vocabularies, the clarity of their explanations, and the complexity of their solutions. Such observations can help you understand their thinking and guide them in developing their reasoning. Your observations can also assist you in adapting the activities for students with special educational needs.

Three different icons appear in the book, as shown in the key. One alerts readers to material quoted from *Principles and Standards for School Mathematics,* another points them to supplementary materials on the CD-ROM that accompanies the book, and a third signals the blackline masters and indicates their locations in the appendix.

Key to Icons

Principles and Standards

CD-ROM

Blackline Master

Although this book emphasizes reasoning and problem solving, it is not intended to be a complete curriculum for developing reasoning methods and problem-solving strategies in fifth grade. We encourage you instead to use it in conjunction with other instructional materials.

The authors gratefully acknowledge the contributions of Marilyn Riggins and Jim Yeatts for their work with Karol Yeatts on Carina's Pet Shop, of Caroline Barrow and Judie Melillo for their work with Michael Battista on Making and Breaking Solids, and of Michelle Chamberlin and Sandra Paull for their collaboration with Judith Zawojewski on Which Month to Ski? Special thanks go the teachers and students at Mount Vernon Elementary School, St. Petersburg, Florida, and Riverside Christian School, Tampa, Florida, for their assistance to Denisse Thompson in field-testing Comparing Ourselves to Others.

Navigations Series

Grade 5

Problem Solving and Reasoning

Introduction

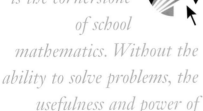
Principles and Standards for School Mathematics (NCTM 2000) states that "problem solving is the cornerstone of school mathematics. Without the ability to solve problems, the usefulness and power of mathematical ideas, knowledge, and skills are severely limited" (p. 182). NCTM continues to emphasize problem solving in the recently released *Curriculum Focal Points for Prekindergarten through Grade 8 Mathematics: A Quest for Coherence* (NCTM 2006). This new publication also stresses the importance of learning mathematical content "in the context of a focused and cohesive curriculum that implements problem solving, reasoning, and critical thinking" (p. 10). Mathematical investigations that challenge students to deal with nonroutine problems and situations should be a regular part of Standards-based instruction at all levels.

Just as solving problems can help students make sense of their changing world, justifying solutions and communicating the results of mathematical investigations can help elementary students develop and expand their reasoning abilities. One goal is for students to develop ways of thinking about mathematics that encourage sense making and reasoning about solutions and strategies. The mathematics classroom is the main environment in which students speak and write mathematics. Hence, it is essential that teachers offer students opportunities to communicate mathematically by having them make, test, discuss, and refine conjectures, ultimately accepting or rejecting them.

The investigations in this book engage students in extended tasks that enable them to look for relationships among concepts in the five content strands enumerated in *Principles and Standards for School Mathematics*:

1

number and operations, algebra, geometry, measurement, and data analysis and probability. Each investigation enables students to focus on one strand in depth. At the same time, the investigations illustrate how a carefully chosen mathematical task can bridge content areas. For example, even though the focus of the data analysis investigation is on analyzing data and drawing conclusions from them, students also work with numerical computations involving averaging and decimal numbers. And although the focus of the algebra investigation is on looking for patterns and writing expressions to describe the data, students also graph the results, combining algebra and data analysis.

Aspects of Problem Solving

Good problems challenge students to develop and apply strategies, serve as a means to introduce new concepts, and offer a context for using skills. Problem solving is not a specific topic to be taught but a process that permeates all mathematics.

What behaviors might a teacher expect to observe in a classroom that makes problem solving a focus? According to *Principles and Standards for School Mathematics*, all students should—

- build new mathematical knowledge through problem solving;
- solve problems that arise in mathematics and in other contexts;
- apply and adapt a variety of appropriate strategies to solve problems; and
- monitor and reflect on the process of mathematical problem solving. (NCTM 2000, p. 402)

The investigations in this book give fifth-grade students an opportunity to engage in problem solving, discuss their ideas and conjectures in pairs or small groups, and justify their thinking to the teacher and other members of the class. As teachers facilitate the investigations, the tasks naturally lead to such questions as "Why?" and "How do you know?"

Students build new mathematical knowledge through problem solving

Students can learn new mathematical concepts and skills through problem solving. A successful problem-centered approach uses interesting problems to motivate students to spend time and energy and be persistent in seeking solutions. Under the guidance of a teacher who encourages students to reason creatively and make connections among ideas, students can discover new mathematical concepts, techniques, and relationships. New ideas often emerge from discussions among students. Teachers should guide such discussions carefully so that the students learn the difference between correct mathematical reasoning and incorrect reasoning and between sound problem-solving strategies and unsound ones. The teacher must summarize classroom discussions so that the students are aware of the new knowledge and skills that they have derived from the problem-solving experience.

Students solve problems that arise in mathematics and other contexts

The investigations in this book pose problems to solve in contexts that are mathematically rich, appeal to fifth graders, and facilitate communication skills.

- In PINs and Other Secret Codes (focusing on number and operations), students explore simple tests of divisibility as they develop a secret code for a personal identification number (PIN) like those that people create and use to gain entry to a home, a bank account, or computer files protected by an electronic security system.

- In Carina's Pet Shop (focusing on algebra), students investigate the patterns and rates of change in pet sales at a newly opened shop. Serving as teams of accountants, they make tables and graphs to help the owner project the demand for particular animals in her shop.

- In Making and Breaking Solids (focusing on geometry), students gain experience in decomposing and recomposing three-dimensional shapes. The accompanying CD-ROM includes an applet, 3-D Shape Decomposition Tool, which students can use to check their work, reinforce their understanding of spatial relationships, and develop their skill in visualizing objects in three-dimensional space.

- In Comparing Ourselves with Others (focusing on measurement), students make and examine a number of measurements, including measurements of some of their own physical attributes (such as the length of an arm). They compare the measurements of their attributes with one another and estimate corresponding measurements for an imaginary giant who is proportioned exactly like themselves.

- In Which Month to Ski? (focusing on data analysis), students interpret a set of data on daily snowfall to determine the month (January–April) that is likely to have the most new snow, thus offering the best skiing conditions at a resort.

In each of these investigations, students grapple with problems that arise in real-world situations. The problems are interesting and challenging vehicles for exploring mathematics and thinking about relationships.

Students apply and adapt a variety of strategies to solve problems

As students explore problems, they need to consider a variety of strategies to investigate the solution. The investigations in this book engage them in a number of different approaches. In Carina's Pet Shop, for example, they represent pet sales by completing tables and plotting points. In Making and Breaking Solids, they work with drawings, manipulatives, and computer software to solve problems. In Which Month to Ski? groups of students use various methods, including averaging, to compare data on daily snowfall for several months, and they represent their work in bar graphs and tables. The varied

"Students who can both develop and carry out a plan to solve a mathematical problem are exhibiting knowledge that is much deeper and more useful than simply carrying out a computation." (NCTM 2000, p. 182)

"Reflecting on different ways of thinking about and representing a problem solution allows comparisons of strategies and consideration of different representations." (NCTM 2000, p. 185)

"Good problems and problem-solving tasks encourage reflection and communication and can emerge from the students' environment or from purely mathematical contexts." (NCTM 2000, p. 183)

representations afford students many ways to explore a problem and enable those with different learning styles to participate in and benefit from the problem-solving experience.

Students monitor and reflect on the process of mathematical problem solving

As students work through good mathematical tasks, they reflect on their work to determine what strategies are effective and where they need to make adjustments. For instance, the investigation PINs and Other Secret Codes calls on students to look for patterns in different number relationships to discover tests for determining when a number is divisible by 2, 3, 4, 5, 6, 8, 9, or 10. In Making and Breaking Solids, students investigate planar cuts to three-dimensional figures to produce other 3-D shapes, developing their visualization skills by making conjectures first and then testing them, sometimes by working with the 3-D Shape Decomposition Tool on the CD-ROM. In Comparing Ourselves with Others, students use a multistep problem-solving process to determine measurements for physical attributes of an imaginary giant: first, they measure the attributes in themselves, then they determine the ratio of their height to the length of their arm, their little finger, their foot, and common objects such as a toothbrush, and finally, they use these ratios to determine the corresponding lengths of a giant's arm, finger, foot, and toothbrush. In Which Month to Ski? students consider different ways to compare daily snowfall in months with different numbers of days and compare the results produced by one method with the results produced by another. In addition, they create an approach that someone could apply to other data sets as new information becomes available. As the students complete all these investigations and others like them, they discover that reflecting on the process they use with one problem can help them build a repertoire of problem-solving strategies that they can apply to a wide range of problems.

Aspects of Reasoning

Reasoning develops over time as teachers facilitate discussion of rich tasks and help students learn "to construct valid arguments and to evaluate the arguments of others" (NCTM 2000, p. 188). As students reason about mathematics, they should—

- make and investigate mathematical conjectures;
- develop and evaluate mathematical arguments and proofs; and
- select and use various types of reasoning and methods of proof. (NCTM 2000, p. 402)

Students make and investigate mathematical conjectures

Students need to learn that making conjectures on the basis of patterns is a natural part of mathematical thinking and problem solving.

The investigation PINs and Other Secret Codes helps students reason, for example, that a number divisible by both *m* and *n* must be divisible by the product *m* × *n* by letting them discover, for instance, that a number divisible by both 2 and 3 is divisible by 6. In Making and Breaking Solids, students think about the properties of geoblocks to make a conjecture about whether the volume of one block is greater than, less than, or equal to the volume of another. Students use relationships among the various blocks to draw conclusions. For instance, if they can put two blocks of type B (see the margin) together to make one block of type A, and they can also put two blocks of type F together to make one block of type A, then block B and block F must have the same volume. In Which Month to Ski? students define "best month to ski" in different ways in relation to the snowfall data that they have. They compare their definitions and determine which they can apply to their own and other data sets.

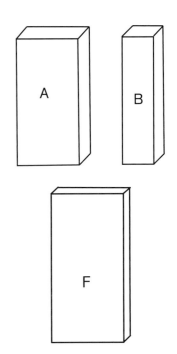

Students develop and evaluate mathematical arguments and proofs

Students in grade 5 should begin to understand that solving problems often involves considering examples, looking for unifying properties and relationships, and expressing these in mathematical statements that they can evaluate. In the investigation Carina's Pet Shop, the students compare different rates of pet sales to determine how many animals the owner will need to have in stock to meet customer demand. To complete an activity in Comparing Ourselves with Others, the students must find an interesting measurement pertaining to an animal, use multiplicative reasoning to compare this measurement to an analogous measurement pertaining to themselves, and explain the comparison that they have made. In Which Month to Ski? students examine data on daily snowfall at a ski resort to develop a process for determining which month, January–April, is best for skiing. They present their process to the class and then adjust it on the basis of feedback from other students.

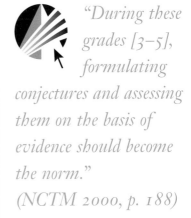

"During these grades [3–5], formulating conjectures and assessing them on the basis of evidence should become the norm."
(NCTM 2000, p. 188)

Students select and use various types of reasoning and methods of proof

By grade 5, students have begun to understand what it means to develop and test conjectures about relationships that hold for many examples. They are learning to express their theories and discoveries in general terms that they can defend with convincing arguments. In working through the investigations in this book, the students explain or justify their reasoning in different ways and contexts. PINS and Other Secret Codes prompts students to reason from examples to discover divisibility tests, which they apply in creating a secret PIN. Carina's Pet Shop guides them in using graphs to compare rates of pet sales. Making and Breaking Solids invites them to reason by making conjectures that they then test by using geoblocks or a computer applet. Comparing Ourselves with Others encourages students to use multiplicative reasoning to make comparisons of two measurements. Which Month to

Ski? calls on students to develop a process and then generalize it to communicate it to someone else for use with additional data.

The Role of the Teacher

As students explore the tasks in this book, their teachers should monitor their activities and foster the interactions necessary to maintain high levels of reasoning (see Stein and Smith [1998], on the CD-ROM). The tasks are mathematically rich, but if teachers provide too many clues or too much specific help early in the process, they can stifle the deep thinking that the tasks require of students. The challenge for teachers is to facilitate students' communication about the task without directing them toward a particular solution.

From detailed observations of an elementary class using a Standards-based curriculum, Fraivillig (2001) has identified various strategies that are essential to helping students think deeply about mathematical ideas and share their thinking with others. These approaches fall into three broad categories: eliciting students' thinking, supporting students' thinking, and extending students' thinking. Descriptions of the strategies in each category are summarized in figure 1.

Fig. 1.
Strategies to advance students' thinking (adapted from Fraivillig [2001], pp. 454–59)

Strategies to elicit students' thinking
- Elicit many solution methods for one problem.
- Wait for, and listen to, students' descriptions of solution methods.
- Encourage students to elaborate and discuss.
- Use students' explanations as a basis for the lesson's content.
- Convey an attitude of acceptance of students' errors and efforts.
- Promote collaborative problem solving.

Strategies to support students' thinking
- Remind students of conceptually similar problems.
- Provide background knowledge.
- Lead students through "instant replays." (Revisit student solutions.)
- Write symbolic representations of solutions when appropriate.

Strategies to extend students' thinking
- Maintain high standards and expectations for all students.
- Encourage students to make generalizations.
- List all solution methods on the board to promote reflection.
- Push individual students to try alternative solution methods.
- Promote the use of more efficient solution methods.

In addition, research from the Quantitative Understanding Amplifying Student Achievement and Reasoning (QUASAR) Project in urban schools with underachieving students found that the following actions by teachers were associated with higher performance by their students on a test of problem solving (Henningsen and Stein 1997; Stein, Grover, and Henningsen 1996; Smith and Stein 1998):

- Teachers press for explanations and meaning.
- Teachers have capable students model high-level performance.
- Teachers allow appropriate time for students to explore the task, think, and make sense of mathematics for themselves.
- Teachers note conceptual connections.
- Teachers build on students' prior knowledge.

Teachers who engage in behaviors like those identified by Fraivillig and the QUASAR researchers can help students develop their reasoning and problem-solving abilities. Teachers can use the following questions to help elicit students' reasoning:

- "Why?"
- "How do you know?"
- "What other problems can you remember that are similar to this one?"
- "Are there other ways you could solve this problem?"
- "Do you agree with this approach to this problem? Why, or why not?"

Such questions can stimulate important teacher-student discourse that will strengthen the reasoning abilities of all students and can involve students in mathematical communication in the classroom.

The role of the teacher is indispensable, and the investigations in this book are designed to help teachers encourage problem solving and reasoning by elementary school mathematics students. Engaging students in these processes is an essential component of developing their mathematical power.

See Fraivillig (2001) on the CD-ROM for classroom strategies that elicit, support, and extend students' thinking.

See Henningsen and Stein (1997), Smith and Stein (1998), and Stein and Smith (1998) on the CD-ROM for ideas on using mathematical tasks to stimulate reflection.

Stein and Smith (1998; available on the CD-ROM) discuss the importance of cultivating habits of reflection on teaching for lifelong professional development.

NAVIGATIONS
SERIES

GRADE 5

PROBLEM SOLVING *and* REASONING

Investigations

PINs and Other Secret Codes

Focus

Reasoning about number relationships

Overview

Students in grade 5 should "understand numbers, ways of representing numbers, relationships among numbers, and number systems" and be able to "describe classes of numbers according to characteristics such as … their factors" (NCTM 2000, p. 148). In this investigation, fifth graders examine the characteristics of numbers that are evenly divisible by 2–10 (except 7) to discover ways of testing whether a number is divisible by each of these divisors. The investigation informally calls these tests of divisibility "rules."

Goals

- Discover divisibility "rules," or tests, for determining whether a number is divisible by the divisors 2–10 (except 7)
- Use these tests of divisibility to understand and solve multiplication and division problems

Mathematical Content

This investigation supports the following Number and Operations and Process Standards and expectations for grades 3–5 (NCTM 2000, pp. 392, 402):

Number and Operations

- Understand numbers, ways of representing numbers, relationships among numbers, and number systems
  - Describe classes of numbers according to characteristics such as … their factors

Problem Solving

- Build new mathematical knowledge through problem solving
- Monitor and reflect on the process of mathematical problem solving

Reasoning and Proof

- Make and investigate mathematical conjectures

In our technological age, bank accounts, computers, alarm systems, and a variety of Web sites require individuals to key in a PIN—a personal identification number—to gain entry or access to information. Remembering all these PINs can become cumbersome. As a result, many people use arithmetic relationships or properties to help them recall their PINs and obtain easy access to their personal accounts.

By using the concept of a PIN and applying divisibility "rules," students strengthen their critical thinking skills and make sense of mathematical reasoning. As they discover ways of testing the divisibility of a certain number by particular divisors, students enhance their sense of number, also reinforcing concepts of place value and an understanding of division. Familiarity with these tests increases students' mathematical power.

Prior Knowledge or Experience

- A grounding in the multiplication tables
- An understanding of the processes of multiplication and division

Materials

For each student—

- A copy of the following blackline masters:
  - "Can You Divide It Evenly?"
  - "How Do You Know It's Divisible?"
  - "A PIN for Mr. Mitchell"
- A calculator
- Paper and pencils

For the teacher—

- An overhead projector (optional)
- Transparencies of each of the following blackline masters (optional):
  - "Can You Divide It Evenly?"
  - "How Do You Know It's Divisible?"
  - "A PIN for Mr. Mitchell"

pp. 78–84; 85–86; 87

Classroom Environment

Students work in pairs to create a secret five- or six-digit personal identification number (PIN) that conforms to specified criteria.

Investigation

This investigation challenges the students to create personal identification numbers (PINs) by applying divisibility "rules," which they develop as informal tests of divisibility rather than as formal rules. To open the investigation, guide your students in exploring the characteristics of numbers that are evenly divisible by the numbers 2–10 (except 7, which the students do not investigate as a divisor in the core investigation). Figure 1 shows these characteristics, which form the basis of related divisibility rules.

Begin this exploration by giving each student a copy of the blackline master "Can You Divide It Evenly?" This activity sheet presents a chart that lists the numbers 1–100 and asks the students to specify which numbers are divisible by which divisors. Have the students work by themselves to enter a "Y" (for *yes*) in any cell that corresponds to an even division. For the sake of visual clarity and readability, have the students leave all the other cells blank (a finished chart appears in the Solutions section).

Fig. **1.**

Divisibility "rules" for divisors 2–10, except 7

Divisor	Characteristic(s) of a number that is evenly divisible by the divisor
2	The number is even. (That is, the units digit is 0, 2, 4, 6, or 8.)
3	The sum of the digits is divisible by 3.
4	The last two digits form a number that is divisible by 4.
5	The units digit is 5 or zero.
6	The number is divisible by both 2 and 3.
8	The last three digits form a number that is divisible by 8. (No example appears on the chart in "Can You Divide It Evenly?" because the only three-digit number is 100.)
9	The sum of all the digits is divisible by 9.
10	The units digit is zero.

After the students have completed the chart, go over their responses as a class, letting them correct any mistakes in their work. Help the students make the following observations about the chart:

- Beginning with 2, every second number is divisible by 2.
- Beginning with 3, every third number is divisible by 3.
- Beginning with 4, every fourth number is divisible by 4.
- Beginning with 5, every fifth number is divisible by 5.
- Beginning with 6, every sixth number is divisible by 6.
- Beginning with 8, every eighth number is divisible by 8.
- Beginning with 9, every ninth number is divisible by 9.
- Beginning with 10, every tenth number is divisible by 10.

Discovering Tests of Divisibility

Next, give each student a copy of the blackline master "How Do You Know It's Divisible?" Have the students continue working together as they use this sheet to consider ways to test divisibility on the basis of the data in their charts on "Can You Divide It Evenly?"

Begin by guiding the students in investigating a rule for 2. Ask the students to look at their charts and pick out five numbers that are divisible by 2. Have them enter their selections as examples in row 2, column 2, of the new chart on "How Do You Know It's Divisible?" Next, on the board or an overhead transparency, write five numbers between 100 and 150. Some of your numbers should be divisible by 2, and some should not. Ask the students to sort these five numbers into those that are divisible by 2 and those that are not. Say, "Enter the numbers that are divisible by 2 as additional examples in your new chart."

Ask the students, "Can you list three more numbers between 100 and 150 that are divisible by 2?" By now, many of your students will probably have noticed that any number that is even is divisible by 2. Ask the students what all their examples have in common, and see if they can suggest a rule for divisibility by 2. Discuss the students' suggestions, and then have the students record the rule for divisibility by 2 in row 2, column 3, of their charts.

Turn the students' attention to numbers that are divisible by 5. To help the students discover a rule for divisibility by 5, follow the same procedure as before:

- Have the students select five examples of numbers divisible by 5 from their first chart and enter them in row for 5, column 2, on their new one.
- Write five more numbers between 100 and 150 on the board or a transparency. (Some of these numbers should be divisible by 5, and others should not.)
- Have the students sort the numbers into those that are divisible by 5 and those that are not, and direct them to enter those that are divisible by 5 as additional examples on their charts.
- Ask the students to list three more examples between 100 and 150 that are divisible by 5.
- Say, "Can you now state a rule for divisibility by 5?" Discuss the students' results, and have them record the rule in row 5, column 3, of their charts.

Repeat the process to help the students discover a divisibility rule for 10. Prompt them to think about the fact that 10 = 2 × 5. To extend their thinking about numbers that are divisible by 10, you could give them the following tasks:

- "List three numbers that are divisible by 2, 5, *and* 10. Tell why these numbers are divisible by all three of these divisors."
- "List three numbers that are divisible by 2 and 5 but not 10". (Give the students time to think why there are no such numbers. Emphasize that 10 equals 2 times 5; therefore, if a number is divisible by 2 and 5, it is also divisible by 10, which is the product of 2 times 5.)"

Use the same process as before to help your students try to discover tests of divisibility for the divisors 3, 4, 6, 8, and 9.

Creating PINs

Give each student a copy of the blackline master "A PIN for Mr. Mitchell." Assign a partner to each student, and read the scenario aloud to all the pairs of students:

Mr. Mitchell has just installed a new security system at his house. He must create a secret six-digit personal identification number, or PIN, as his password for the system. He decides to use the six digits in his date of birth: 05-24-76. It is very important to Mr. Mitchell that no one else discover his PIN, so he decides to rearrange the digits in a six-digit number that no one is likely to guess. After much thought, Mr. Mitchell decides to rearrange the numerals so that, from the left—

- the first digit is the largest of all the digits;
- the number formed by the first two digits is divisible by 2;

See Bennett and Nelson (2002) on the CD-ROM for the use of base-ten blocks to verify and illustrate divisibility rules.

- the number formed by the first three digits is divisible by 3;
- the number formed by the first four digits is divisible by 4;
- the number formed by the first five digits is divisible by 5; and
- the entire six-digit number is divisible by 6.

The activity sheet tells the students that Mr. Mitchell needs their help in creating a six-digit number that meets all of these conditions. By using the six digits in Mr. Mitchell's date of birth, can they create an acceptable PIN for him?

Encourage the students to consider the possibilities for each digit of Mr. Mitchell's PIN. Seven arrangements of the digits will satisfy Mr. Mitchell's conditions, so all your student pairs are unlikely to come up with the same number. A description follows of the process of arriving at one satisfactory arrangement and testing it step by step:

1. Of all the numbers in Mr. Mitchell's date of birth, 7 is the largest. Therefore, the first digit in the PIN must be 7.
2. The number formed by the first and second digits must be divisible by 2. The selection of zero as the second digit satisfies this condition: 70 is divisible by 2 because 70 is an even number.
3. The number formed by the first, second, and third digits must be divisible by 3. The selection of 2 as the third digit satisfies this condition: 702 is divisible by 3 because the sum of the digits (7 + 0 + 2 = 9) is divisible by 3.
4. The number formed by the first, second, third, and fourth digits must be divisible by 4. The selection of 4 as the fourth digit satisfies this condition: 7024 is divisible by 4 because the last 2 digits (24) are divisible by 4.
5. The number formed by the first, second, third, fourth, and fifth digits must be divisible by 5. The selection of 5 as the fifth digit satisfies this condition: 70245 is divisible by 5 because the last digit is 5.
6. The number formed by the first, second, third, fourth, fifth, and sixth digits must be divisible by 6. The selection of 6 as the sixth digit satisfies this condition: 702456 is divisible by 6 because it is divisible by both 2 and 3. It is divisible by 2 because it ends in an even number. It is divisible by 3 because the sum of the digits (7 + 0 + 2 + 4 + 5 + 6 = 24) is divisible by 3. Thus, the entire six-digit number is divisible by 6.

So the number 702456 satisfies all of Mr. Mitchell's conditions.

The other arrangements of the six digits that will satisfy the same conditions follow:

720456

726054

726450

762450

762054

765204

On the board or an overhead transparency, list these possible PINs for Mr. Mitchell (including in your list the PIN discussed above, 702456), and guide your students in making observations about them. All the numbers, of course, begin with 7, because it is the largest digit. Be sure that the students recognize that the second digit, which gives a two-digit number that must be divisible by 2, is even, and thus the candidates for consideration are 0, 2, 4, or 6. But when the students consider the third condition—that the first three digits must be divisible by 3—they should quickly realize that the second digit cannot be a 4. For a number to be divisible by 3, the sum of its digits must also be divisible by 3. Let the students consider the possibilities with 4 as the second digit:

$$7 + 4 + 0 = 11$$
$$7 + 4 + 2 = 13$$
$$7 + 4 + 5 = 16$$
$$7 + 4 + 6 = 17$$

None of these sums is divisible by 3, so 4 is a "dead end" and cannot be a choice for the second digit.

Likewise, zero soon proves to be a dead end as the second digit in all cases except one—702456. Again, have the students consider the possibilities:

$$7 + 0 + 2 = 9$$
$$7 + 0 + 4 = 11$$
$$7 + 0 + 5 = 12$$
$$7 + 0 + 6 = 13$$

Two of these sums are divisible by 3: 9 and 12. So initially the students may consider 702_ _ _ and 705_ _ _ as possible PINs for Mr. Mitchell. Encourage them to see, however, that when they get to the fifth condition and need a five-digit number that is divisible by 5, they will be at an impasse if they have already used both zero and 5—the only digits that can serve as the fifth digit in Mr. Mitchell's PIN.

Point out that every even arrangement of all six digits is divisible by 6. This is true because every even arrangement satisfies both conditions of the divisibility test for 6. Evenness guarantees divisibility by 2, and since the sum of all six digits is always 24, as guaranteed by the commutative property of addition, and 24 is divisible by 3, every arrangement of the six digits is divisible by 3. Thus, every even arrangement satisfies both conditions for divisibility by 6.

Next, have the students continue to work in pairs to create a secret five- or six-digit PIN that satisfies a sequence of conditions about the divisibility of the digits in the same way that Mr. Mitchell's PIN does. Working with paper and pencil, they should write their conditions and a PIN that satisfies them and verify their work by applying divisibility tests.

Ask each pair of students to share the conditions that they have set for the digits in their PIN. Let the other students use these conditions as clues to try to discover the PIN.

Extension

To enrich your students' understanding, you might share with your students the conventional tests for determining whether a number is divisible by 7 or 11. Then you could let them test various numbers with the algorithms. If you have students who are especially inquisitive about mathematics, you could challenge them to spend a little time probing why the tests work. The full explanations, however, are beyond the grasp of most fifth graders.

The test for divisibility by 7 is usually given as follows:

> Double the units digit of the number that you are testing, and then subtract this product from the remaining digits. If the new number that you obtain is divisible by 7, then your original number is also divisible by 7.

If the number that a student is testing is large, he or she can repeat the process until it produces a number that clearly is or is not divisible by 7 (fig. 2 illustrates and explains the process for two sample numbers). Note that the algorithm actually involves repeated subtraction of multiples of 7. If the number that remains is divisible by 7, then so is the original number. (Bennett and Nelson [2002] on the CD-ROM present an alternative divisibility test for 7; students may find that test easier to understand.)

Fig. **2.**

Two examples, with explanations, of the process for determining whether a number is divisible by 7

Students can consider rules for divisibility by 2, 4, 5, and 10 in the context of the children's book *One Hundred Hungry Ants* (Pinczes 1993), which tells the story of one hundred ants marching in single file to a picnic. On the way, they decide that they could go faster in two lines of fifty, then faster still in four lines of twenty-five, and still faster in ten lines of ten. So much frantic reorganizing delays the ants, and they miss the picnic!

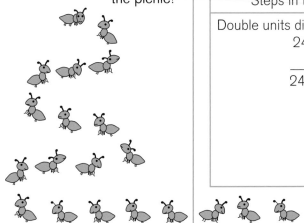

Test for divisibility by 7 applied to 4074

Steps in the algorithm	Explanation of the process
Double units digit and subtract: 4074̸ − 8 ―――― 399	Actually subtracting 4074 − 84 (= 12 × 7) ―――― 3990
	3990 = 399 × 10, so 7 divides 3990 only if 7 divides 399; thus, we can test 399:
Repeat the process on 399: 39̸9̸ −18 ―――― 21	Actually subtracting 399 −189 (= 27 × 7) ―――― 210
21 is clearly divisible by 7, so 4074 is also divisible by 7: 4074 = 582 × 7.	210 = 21 × 10. Since 21 is divisible by 7, so are 399 and 4074.

Test for divisibility by 7 applied to 24,283

Steps in the algorithm	Explanation of the process
Double units digit and subtract: 24283̸ − 6 ―――― 2422	Actually subtracting 24283 − 63 (= 9 × 7) ―――― 24220
	24220 = 2422 × 10, so 7 divides 24220 only if 7 divides 2422; thus, we can test 2422:

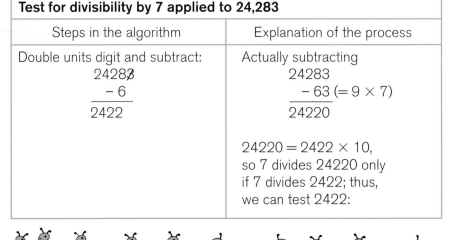

Fig. **2.** (continued)

Steps in the algorithm	Explanation of the process
Repeat the process on 2422: 24 2 2̸ − 4 ————— 238	Actually subtracting 2422 − 42 (= 6 × 7) ————— 2380 2380 = 238 × 10, so 7 divides 2380 only if 7 divides 238; thus, we can test 238:
Repeat the process on 238: 23 8̸ −16 ————— 7	Actually subtracting 238 −168 (= 24 × 7) ————— 70
7 is obviously divisible by 7, so 24,283 is also divisible by 7: 24,283 = 3,469 × 7.	70 = 10 × 7. Since 70 is divisible by 7, so are 238, 2422, and 24,283.

The test for divisibility by 11 is usually explained as follows:

Starting with the units digit of the number that you are testing, alternately subtract and add the remaining digits, working from right to left. If your result is divisible by 11, then the original number is also divisible by 11.

Figure 3 illustrates this process for two sample numbers. Though the explanation of why this test works (see fig. 4) is too complex for most fifth graders, you may find that a thorough understanding of the algorithm is helpful to you as your students use it to test numbers for divisibility by 11.

Test for divisibility by 11 applied to 2,673

$3 - 7 + 6 - 2 = 0$

Since 0 is divisible by 11, so is 2,673 (2,673 = 243 × 11).

Test for divisibility by 11 applied to 41,316

$6 - 1 + 3 - 1 + 4 = 11$

Since 11 is divisible by 11, so is 41,316 (41,316 = 3,756 × 11).

Fig. **3.**

Two examples of the process of determining whether a number is divisible by 11

Assessment

Much of your assessment of your students' understanding will be informal, as you observe the students at work. For a written assessment, you might have your students work on their own to write divisibility

Fig. **4.**

An explanation of the test for
divisibility by 11

Let a, b, c, d, e, and f be the digits in a six-digit number $abcdef$.

Thus, $abcdef = (100{,}000)(a) + (10{,}000)(b) + (1{,}000)(c) + (100)(d) + (10)(e) + (1)(f)$.

Observe the following pattern:

$10 = 11 - 1$	$(1 \times 11 = 11)$
$100 = 99 + 1$	$(9 \times 11 = 99)$
$1000 = 1001 - 1$	$(91 \times 11 = 1001)$
$10000 = 9999 + 1$	$(909 \times 11 = 9999)$
$100000 = 100001 - 1$	$(9091 \times 11 = 11)$

And so on …

Use this pattern to rewrite the given number:
$abcdef = (100{,}001 - 1)(a) + (9999 + 1)(b) + (1001 - 1)(c) + (99 + 1)(d) + (11 - 1)(e) + f = [(100{,}001)(a) + (9999)(b) + (1001)(c) + (99)(d) + (11)(e)] + [-a + b - c + d - e + f]$

The sum $(100{,}001)(a) + (9999)(b) + (1001)(c) + (99)(d) + (11)(e)$ is clearly divisible by 11.

Thus, the number $abcdef$ is divisible by 11 if the sum $-a + b - c + d - e + f$, or $f - e + d - c + b - a$, is also divisible by 11.

conditions for a new PIN. You can have them exchange their conditions with a partner and closely observe how well the students apply tests of divisibility to discover a PIN that satisfies the conditions. You might also consider inviting your students to present this investigation to another fifth-grade class.

Reflections

By testing various numbers for divisibility by particular divisors, students can begin a very useful process of categorizing numbers by their characteristics. Fifth-grade students will find this investigation challenging and thought provoking. Reflecting on why these tests of divisibility work can reinforce students' ideas about factors, even and odd numbers, place value, and number patterns, as well as their basic understanding of multiplication and division.

Connections

This investigation of divisibility "rules" allows students to use the language of mathematics to discover the connection between content and process for the operation of division. Understanding division is a key skill that enables students to comprehend computation with whole numbers, rational numbers, and decimals.

Carina's Pet Shop

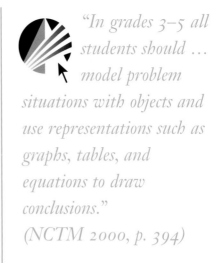

Focus

Reasoning about algebraic relationships

Overview

Students in fifth grade are becoming accustomed to using variables—represented graphically as squares, letters of the alphabet, or other symbols—to express algebraic thinking. They use graphs, tables, and equations to represent relationships, and they construct models of problems and use them to make predictions and draw conclusions. Fifth graders should begin to understand that models are not perfect replicas of problems but approximations that enable them to use mathematics and write equations that lead to acceptable solutions. This investigation helps students understand how a change in one quantity produces a change in a second. To understand the mathematical idea of change, students must understand the relationship between the rate of change in one variable and the rate of change in another.

Goals

- Represent data by creating tables
- Represent data by constructing graphs
- Understand how graphs represent change
- Represent change as an algebraic expression

Mathematical Content

This investigation promotes the following Algebra and Process Standards and expectations for grades 3–5 (NCTM 2000, pp. 394, 402).

Algebra

- Understand patterns, relations, and functions
  - Represent and analyze patterns and functions, using words, tables, and graphs
- Use mathematical models to represent and understand quantitative relationships
  - Model problem situations with objects and use representations such as graphs, tables, and equations to draw conclusions
- Analyze change in various contexts
  - Investigate how a change in one variable relates to a change in a second variable
  - Identify and describe situations with constant … rates of change and compare them

Problem Solving

- Apply and adapt a variety of appropriate strategies to solve problems

Communication

- Organize and consolidate … mathematical thinking through communication

Representation

- Create and use representations to organize, record, and communicate mathematical ideas

- Select, apply, and translate among mathematical representations to solve problems

- Use representations to model and interpret physical, social, and mathematical phenomena

Students in grades 3–5 should have opportunities to investigate different patterns of change, including change that occurs at a constant rate and change whose rate increases or decreases over time. Fifth-grade students should be encouraged to use models of representation, such as tables and graphs, as they explore and analyze change in various contexts. "This work is a precursor to later, more focused attention on what the slope of a line represents, that is, what the steepness of the line shows about the rate of change" (NCTM 2000, p. 163).

Prior Knowledge or Experience

- Experience in examining patterns

- Experience in setting up data tables

- Experience in plotting points and constructing bar graphs

Materials

For each student—

- A copy of each of the following blackline masters:
  - "Carina's Pet Sales"
  - "Projecting from Patterns"
  - "Animal Accounting"

pp. 88; 89; 90; 91–93

For each pair of students—

- Four sheets of grid paper made from the template "Centimeter Grid Paper" (available as a blackline master)

- Pencils or fine-point markers in three colors

- Two or three sheets of regular paper, lined or unlined

Classroom Environment

After the opening scenario is presented to the whole class, the students work in pairs to investigate Carina's actual and projected sales in her new pet shop. Each pair of students shares its tables and graphs with the rest of the class. The class then discusses each pair's work and investigates the idea of *rate of change*.

Investigation

Give each student a copy of the blackline master "Carina's Pet Sales."
Read the scenario aloud to the class:

Carina opened a pet store in town three weeks ago. Since her
shop opened, she has seen her sales of guinea pigs, gerbils,
and hamsters increase each week. Pet-store owners in other
towns have told Carina that she can expect sales of these pets
to continue increasing for the next five weeks as her shop
becomes established. Carina wants to figure out how many
guinea pigs, gerbils, and hamsters she is likely to sell over the
next five weeks so that she can stock appropriate numbers of
pets of each type.

The activity page explains that Carina knows how many guinea pigs
she has sold in each of the first three weeks. Notes in her records
(shown in the margin) indicate that she sold two guinea pigs in the first
week, four guinea pigs in the second week, and six guinea pigs in the
third week. On the basis of information from other pet-store owners,
Carina expects her weekly sales of guinea pigs to increase at the same
rate for the next five weeks.

Moreover, Carina's notes show that in each of the first three weeks
that her store has been in business, she has sold three times as many
gerbils as guinea pigs and half as many hamsters as gerbils. Other pet-
store owners have told Carina that she can also expect these patterns to
continue over the next five weeks. Tell your students that Carina is
beginning to wonder whether she will be able to stock enough guinea
pigs, gerbils, and hamsters to satisfy her customers' demands for these
pets.

Explain that Carina needs help in projecting the number of pets that
she is likely to sell each week for the next five weeks. Give each student
a copy of the blackline master "Projecting from Patterns." (Be sure that
each student still has a copy of the first sheet, "Carina's Pet Sales"; they
will need to refer to Carina's notes on the sheet.) Assign a partner to
each student, and ask each pair of students to act as a team of accountants to assist Carina in making projections.

Say, "As Carina's new accountants, you must complete the tables on
'Projecting from Patterns.' Look back at Carina's notes about her sales
in the first three weeks as you make predictions and complete these
tables."

Also distribute to each pair of students three sheets of centimeter
grid paper and colored pencils or fine-tipped markers in three colors.
Say, "Carina wants more than tables. She wants coordinate graphs that
show the number of guinea pigs, gerbils, and hamsters that she has
actually sold in the first three weeks and the number that she can expect
to sell during the next five weeks." Direct the students to use the grid
paper and colored pencils or markers to make three coordinate graphs,
using one color to represent each type of pet in the different graphs.
Figures 5, 6, and 7 show tables and graphs of Carina's actual pet sales
for weeks 1–3 and projected sales for weeks 4–8.

If necessary, guide the students in setting up their coordinate graphs.
After they draw their axes, help them determine what the axes will

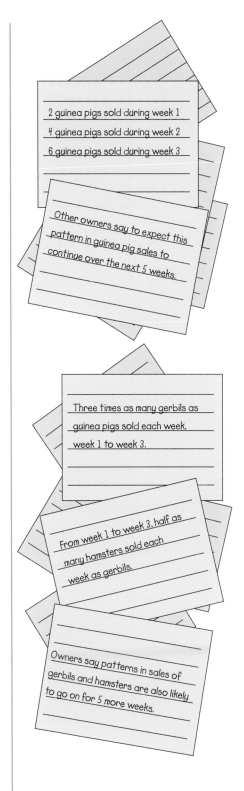

2 guinea pigs sold during week 1

4 guinea pigs sold during week 2

6 guinea pigs sold during week 3

Other owners say to expect this
pattern in guinea pig sales to
continue over the next 5 weeks.

Three times as many gerbils as
guinea pigs sold each week,
week 1 to week 3.

From week 1 to week 3, half as
many hamsters sold each
week as gerbils.

Owners say patterns in sales of
gerbils and hamsters are also likely
to go on for 5 more weeks.

Week	Guinea Pig Sales
1	2
2	4
3	6
4	8
5	10
6	12
7	14
8	16

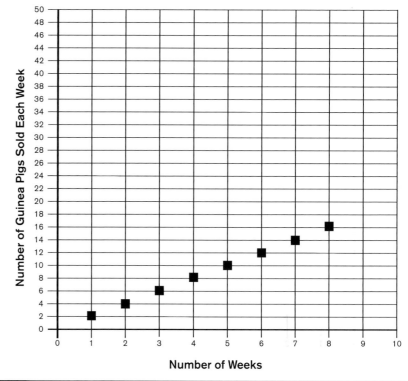

Fig. **5.**

A table and graph showing Carina's actual and projected weekly sales of guinea pigs for weeks 1–8

Week	Gerbil Sales
1	6
2	12
3	18
4	24
5	30
6	36
7	42
8	48

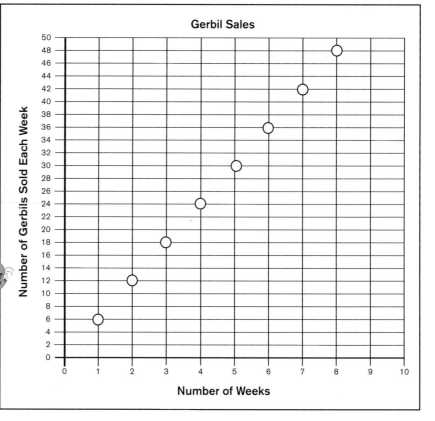

Fig. **6.**

A table and graph showing Carina's actual and projected weekly sales of gerbils for weeks 1–8

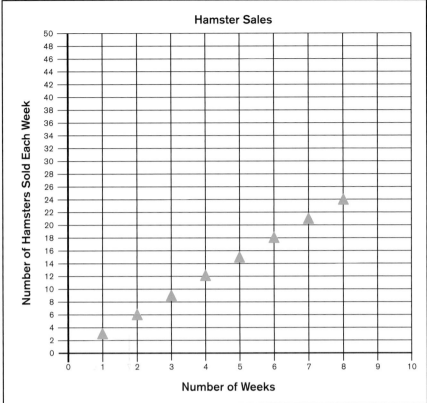

Hamster Sales

Week	Hamster Sales
1	3
2	6
3	9
4	12
5	15
6	18
7	21
8	24

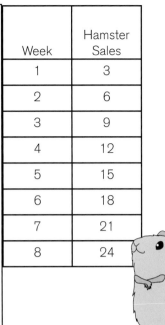

Fig. **7.**

A table and graph showing Carina's actual and projected weekly sales of hamsters for weeks 1–8

show. (Having all the students use the axes in the same way will make comparisons easier.) Say, "Let the horizontal axis [or *x*-axis] show the number of weeks." Give the students time to label the axis, and then say, "Use the vertical axis [or *y*-axis] to show the number of sales each week of guinea pigs, or gerbils, or hamsters, depending on which graph you are making." Again, give the students time to label the axis. Be sure that that they title their graphs and establish uniform scales when they calibrate the axes. Tell the students to select one of their pencils or markers and make colored dots to show sales of a particular pet in particular weeks.

Refer to the colored dots as *data points* to accustom the students to naming them in this way. Ask, "Do you think you should connect the data points on your graph?" If the students say that they should, explain that connecting the segments would not make a meaningful picture of the information. There are no data between the dots—Carina would never be selling fractional parts of guinea pigs as pets! Explain that these graphs represent *discrete* data (which are countable in whole numbers), not *continuous* data. When data are continuous, we can connect the data points on a graph, and we understand that between any two points on the line, there is always another point.

If you need to limit the time that you spend on the activity, you can reduce the number of tables and graphs that each pair of students makes. Assign each pair of students just one type of pet—guinea pigs, gerbils, or hamsters. Tell them, "You are going to construct a table and graph to represent both the actual and the projected sales of your assigned pet for the first eight weeks in which Carina's pet shop is in business."

Depending on your students' experience and abilities, you might prefer to have the students set up their own tables rather than fill in those on the activity page "Projecting from Patterns." If so, provide the student pairs with paper for the creation of tables.

Observe your students as they work on the tables and graphs. You may need to assist them as they determine and plot the weekly sales of gerbils and hamsters. Help them see that on the graph showing guinea pig sales, they plot the ordered pairs (1, 2), (2, 4), and (3, 6) for weeks 1–3. If necessary, explain that an ordered pair gives the "address" of a point on a coordinate grid. The first number tells how far the point is from zero in the horizontal direction, and the second number tells how far it is from zero in the vertical direction. The first number is the x-value of the point, and the second number is its y-value.

The students should see that to obtain the number of gerbils sold in a specific week, they must multiply the number of guinea pig sales for that week by 3. So on the graph showing gerbil sales, they will plot the ordered pairs (1, 6), (2, 12), and (3, 18) for weeks 1–3. To obtain the number of hamsters sold in a specific week, they must divide the number of gerbil sales by 2. So on the graph showing hamster sales, they will plot the ordered pairs (1, 3), (2, 6), and (3, 9).

After the students have completed their work, have each pair share its tables and graphs with the class and discuss the projected sales for weeks 4–8. Help them analyze their work. Say, "Place a straightedge against your plotted points. What do you notice?" When the students point out that the dots, or data points, line up, explain that the relationship between the number of weeks and the number of guinea pigs (or gerbils or hamsters) sold each week is *linear*, even though they should not connect the dots to draw the line in the graph.

When all the pairs have shared their tables and graphs, give each pair a new sheet of grid paper and have the students assemble all the data in one table and one graph. Figure 8 shows a composite table and graph for the sales, actual and projected, of all three pets in weeks 1–8.

Helping students understand a rate of change

Have the students work as a class to examine their composite graphs and explore the idea of *rate of change*. They should notice that Carina's actual and projected sales of guinea pigs, gerbils, and hamsters increase at constant rates. Say, "You used a pattern in Carina's sales of guinea pigs over the first three weeks to complete your tables and make your graphs for the first eight weeks. Can you describe that pattern?" (Carina sold two guinea pigs in week 1, and her guinea pig sales increase by two each week.)

In the same way, ask the students about the patterns in the sales of gerbils and hamsters. (Carina sold six gerbils in week 1, and her gerbil sales increase by six each week; she sold three hamsters in week 1, and her hamster sales increase by three each week.)

Have the students make comparisons among Carina's sales of all three types of pets. Ask, "How do Carina's sales of guinea pigs compare with her sales of gerbils?" (The pet shop sells three times as many gerbils as guinea pigs each week, so Carina's sales of guinea pigs amount to only one-third of her sales of gerbils.) Then ask, "How do Carina's sales of gerbils compare with her sales of hamsters?" (The shop sells half as

An ordered pair gives the "address" of a point on a coordinate grid. The first number tells how far the point is from zero in a horizontal direction, and the second number tells how far it is from zero in a vertical direction. The first number is the x-value of the point, and the second number is its y-value.

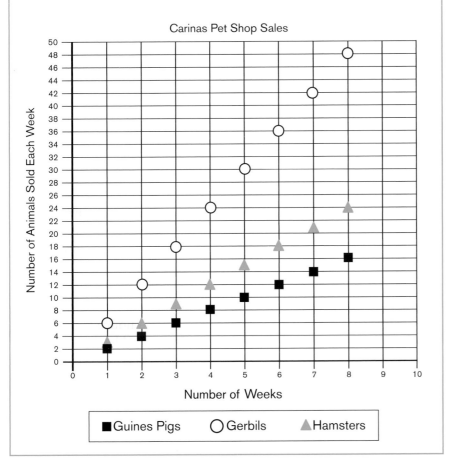

Week	Guinea Pig Sales	Gerbill Sales	Hamster Sales
1	2	6	3
2	4	12	6
3	6	18	9
4	8	24	12
5	10	30	15
6	12	36	18
7	14	42	21
8	16	48	24

Carinas Pet Shop Sales

Number of Animals Sold Each Week

Number of Weeks

■ Guines Pigs   ○ Gerbils   ▲ Hamsters

Fig. **8.**

A composite table and composite graph showing Carina's actual and projected weekly sales of guinea pigs, gerbils, and hamsters for weeks 1–8

many hamsters as gerbils each week, so Carina makes twice as many gerbil sales as hamster sales.)

Guide the students in thinking about the idea of a *rate of change*. Point out that the tables and graphs show two *variables*—that is, two quantities whose values change. Mathematically, we say that the variable that we select first (here, *Number of weeks*) is the *independent* variable, and we call the variable that we determine second, and pair with the first variable, the *dependent* variable (here, *Number of pets sold each week*). The

Students in fifth grade should begin to understand that a variable *is a quantity whose value can change.*

value of this variable *depends on* the value of the first variable. Tell the students, "We call the number of weeks the *independent variable* because we start with a value for this variable—1, 2, 3, 4, 5, 6, 7, or 8. This value simply tells us how many weeks Carina's pet shop has been in business." The students should observe that the value of the independent variable continues increasing week by week, up to week 8.

Then say, "We call the number of pets sold the *dependent variable* because its value *depends on* the value of the first variable—the number of weeks. The dependent variable—the number of pets sold in a week—also increases from week to week." It is very important that students grasp the next idea: "*How* the dependent variable changes in relation to the independent variable is called the *rate of change*." Tell the students that they can determine the rate of change by inspecting the graphs that they have made.

Explain that the dependent variable is often represented as *y*, and the *y*-values are displayed along the vertical axis of the graph. The independent variable is usually represented as *x*, and the *x*-values are displayed along the horizontal axis of the graph.

Say to your students, "Think about Carina's sales of guinea pigs. Your table and graph (see fig. 5) contain all the information you would need to describe the rate of change in guinea pig sales." Have the students inspect their graphs of guinea pig sales and imagine how these graphs would look if the students *did* connect the plotted data points with a line. Explain that such a connecting line would be the "slant line," and its slope would reflect the rate of change in the data.

A line's *slope* represents the ratio of the change in the value of *y* to a corresponding change in the value of *x*. Slope is customarily expressed as a fraction, with a change in *x* in the denominator and the corresponding change in *y* in the numerator: $slope = \dfrac{\Delta y}{\Delta x}$.

Figure 9 shows how your students can use a graph of guinea pig sales to determine the slope of the linear relationship that the graph shows. Have the students select two data points—for example, the points for weeks 2 and 3. Say, "The ordered pairs of values for these points—their "addresses"—are (2, 4) and (3, 6)." Write these ordered pairs on the board. Direct the students to locate the *x*-values of these pairs, 2 and 3, on the *x*-axis. Ask, "From week 2 to week 3, the independent variable (*Number of weeks*) increases by how much?" (1) On the board, write this change of 1 as the denominator of a fraction for the slope: $\dfrac{\square}{1}$.

Next, turn the students' attention to the *y*-values that correspond to these *x*-values. Ask, "In going from week 2 to week 3, the change in the *x*-value is 1, but what is the change in the *y*-value?" (2) To aid the students in giving the correct answer, have them imagine that they can travel only on grid lines from the point (2, 4) to the point (3, 6), as shown in figure 9. Say, "Of course, you would move just one unit horizontally, but how many units would you move vertically?" (2) Explain: "You moved 2 units along the *y*-axis because Carina's guinea pig sales increased by 2 from week 2 to week 3." Tell the students that this number, 2, gives them the value of the numerator in the fraction for

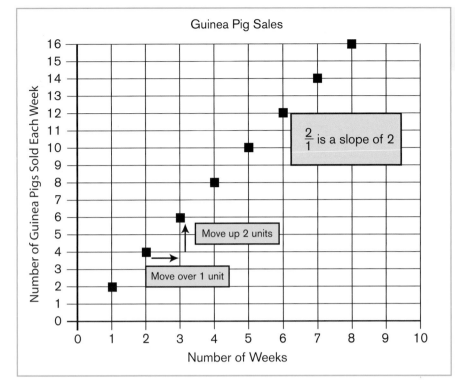

Fig. **9.**

The increase in guinea pig sales from week 2 to week 3

the slope: $\frac{2}{1}$. The numerator shows the change in the number of guinea pig sales in relation to a change in the number of weeks from one week to the next.

Point out to the students that if they moved on grid lines from the data point for week 4 to the data point to week 6, they would move 2 units horizontally and 4 units vertically. The ratio of this change in y-values to the corresponding change in x-values would be $\frac{4}{2}$, which is equivalent to $\frac{2}{1}$. The slope thus remains the same.

The students should see that the relationship of the sales of guinea pigs each week to the number of weeks results in a slope, or rate of change, of 2, since every week the number of guinea pigs sold is 2 more than the previous week. Therefore, as the time variable increases by 1, the guinea pig sales increase by 2. From week 4 to week 6, the time variable increases by 2 and the sales variable increases by 4, and the ratio of the sales variable to the time variable still gives a slope of 2.

Ask the students, "Can you describe the slope, or rate of change, for the sales of gerbils?" Have the students look at their tables and graphs for gerbil sales (see fig. 6). To travel on grid lines from one data point to the next, they must move one unit horizontally and six units vertically, for a slope, or rate of change, of $\frac{6}{1}$, or 6.

Ask, "Can you describe the slope, or rate of change, for Carina's sales of hamsters?" Have the students inspect their tables and graphs for hamster sales (see fig. 7). They should see that to travel on grid lines from one data point to the next, they must move one unit horizontally and three units vertically, for a slope, or rate of change, of $\frac{3}{1}$, or 3.

Carina's Guinea Pig Sales Week by Week

Week	Guinea Pig Sales
1	2
2	4
3	6
4	8
5	10
6	12
7	14
8	16
18	?
20	?
n	$2n$

Carina's Gerbil Sales Week by Week

Week	Gerbil Sales
1	6
2	12
3	18
4	24
5	30
6	36
7	42
8	48
18	?
20	?
n	$6n$

The students may also recognize that the rate of change for Carina's gerbil sales (6) is three times the rate of change of her guinea pig sales (2) and two times the rate of change of her hamster sales (3). Emphasize that the students' composite graphs (see figure 8) show direct relationships among the rates of change. Also be sure that your students understand that these slopes do not change; they are all constant.

Helping students express a rate of change algebraically

The relationship between a change in the independent variable, *Number of weeks*, and a corresponding change in the dependent variable, *Number of sales each week*, may become clearer to the students if they think about rates of change algebraically. Give each student a copy of the blackline master "Animal Accounting" and have the students fill in answers for numbers 1 and 2 while the class discusses them. The students will need to have their completed copies of "Projecting from Patterns" available in front of them.

Question 1 on "Animal Accounting" asks the students to inspect the tables they made to show Carina's weekly sales of guinea pigs on "Projecting from Patterns" (see the upper left margin). Say, "Look at the numbers for the weeks and the numbers of guinea pigs sold during each week. Can you describe the relationship between any particular number of weeks and the corresponding number of guinea pigs sold in that week?"

In addition to noting that Carina's guinea pig sales increase by 2 each week, the students should note that they can determine a week's guinea pig sales by multiplying the number of the week by 2. Say, "Let's call the number of the week n." Point out that question 1 on "Animal Accounting" asks the students what mathematical expression they can write, using n, for the number of guinea pig sales in week n. The students might suggest $2 \times n$, or $n \times 2$. Explain that $2n$ is algebraic shorthand for these expressions. Give the students time to write "$2n$" as the answer to question 1(*a*) on the activity sheet.

Also explain that since Carina expects the pattern of sales to continue through, but not beyond, week 8, n must be between 1 and 8. If the notation "$1 \leq n \leq 8$" would be meaningful to your students, you can show it to them.

Note that the table for the guinea pig sales in the upper left margin includes rows for weeks 18 and 20. Carina has been told that she can expect her sales rates to continue only through week 8. Point out that on "Animal Accounting," however, question 2 asks the students to suppose for the moment that Carina has learned that she can actually expect the rate of change from the first eight weeks to continue through week 20. Have the students project the guinea pig sales for weeks 18 and 20. (36 and 40, respectively) Question 2(*a*) asks them about the guinea pig sales for week 18, and question 2(*b*) calls on them to tell how they found their answer. Give the students time to answer questions 2(*a*) and 2(*b*) on the activity page.

Next, have the students inspect the tables that they completed to show Carina's weekly gerbil sales on "Projecting from Patterns" (see the lower right margin). They should notice that the gerbil sales increase by 6 each week and that if they multiply the number of weeks by 6, they can determine the number of gerbil sales for any week. If they again let n stand for the number of the week, they can write the algebraic expression $6n$ to describe the number of gerbil sales each week. Give the students time to write "$6n$" as the answer to question 1(b) on the activity sheet.

Again, have the students suppose that Carina has learned that she can actually expect gerbil sales to continue to increase at the same rate through week 20. Can they use the algebraic expression $6n$ for the number of gerbil sales in a week to project the gerbil sales for weeks 18 and 20? (108 and 120, respectively) Question 2(c) asks for the number of gerbil sales in week 20, and question 2(d) calls for an explanation of their answer. Let the students answer these questions on the activity sheet.

Now have the students examine the tables that they completed to show Carina's weekly hamster sales on "Projecting from Patterns" (see the margin). The students should notice that Carina's hamster sales increase by 3 each week and that if they multiply the number of weeks by 3 they can determine the number of hamster sales for a week. They can write the algebraic expression $3n$ to describe the relationship in the table. Give the students time to enter this expression as the answer to 1(c) on the activity sheet.

As before, ask the students to suppose that Carina can actually expect sales to continue to increase at this rate through week 20. Can the students project Carina's hamster sales for weeks 18 and 20? (54 and 60, respectively; the activity sheet doesn't ask for either of these projections)

Next, give the students time to complete question 3 on "Animal Accounting" on their own. Here they inspect three graphs (see fig. 10) that represent sales patterns for other pets that Carina sells. The students must match each graph to a description of a situation in Carina's shop.

Graph 1 shows that Carina sells garden snakes at a rate (2 per week) that is constant but neither increasing nor decreasing. Such sales are often described as "flat."

Graph 2 shows Carina's sales of ten kittens that someone left at her door at the beginning of week 4. These sales decreased at a constant rate over the next four weeks. The graph shows a negative slope ($\frac{-1}{1}$, or -1). Though your students should be able to match the situation to the graph without understanding that the slope is negative, you can decide whether they are ready for an explanation of this concept.

Graph 3 depicts Carina's sales of baby rabbits in the five weeks before and the three weeks after Easter. The students should notice that up until Easter Carina's sales of rabbits were brisk and increased at a constant rate. In the week immediately after Easter, her sales of rabbits dropped way down, but in the next two weeks leading up to the eight-week mark, rabbit sales slowly increased, at a much lower constant rate. Before Easter, the slope of the linear relationship is $\frac{4}{1}$; in the sixth week (right after Easter), it is $\frac{-12}{1}$; and in the seventh and eighth weeks, it is $\frac{1}{1}$.

Carina's Hamster Sales Week by Week	
Week	Hamster Sales
1	3
2	6
3	9
4	12
5	15
6	18
7	21
8	24
18	?
20	?
n	$3n$

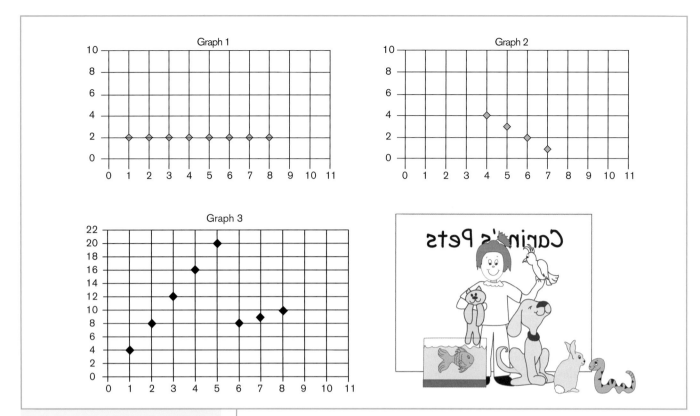

Fig. **10.**

Graphs of three other sales situations at Carina's pet shop

Extension

As an extension activity, present this additional scenario to the students:

> Carina's pet shop did so well in its first three weeks that at the beginning of week 4 Carina added goldfish to her stock. At the end of a week, Carina checked her records and found that she had sold 9 goldfish. In the next week, she sold 18 goldfish, and in the week after that, she sold 27 goldfish. At that point, Carina wondered if soon she would be selling more goldfish than gerbils! Of course, she remembered that other pet-store owners had told her to expect her sales rates to continue to increase at the same rates only through week 8, when her shop would no longer be new. But if Carina's goldfish sales continued at the same pace through week 8, would they pass her gerbil sales by then?

Have the students use paper and pencil and work in pairs or on their own to create tables and graphs showing actual and projected sales of both gerbils and goldfish through week 8 (see fig. 11). Encourage the students to refer to the tables and graphs that they made for Carina's gerbil sales on "Projecting from Patterns." Remind the students that Carina can expect her gerbil sales to increase at a constant rate of 6 each week over the first 8 weeks. Emphasize that Carina began selling goldfish during week 4, so the students should begin recording the number of goldfish that Carina has sold each week in row 4 of a new column on the table.

After the students have completed their tables and graphs, ask them to discuss the results. (They should find that in the fourth week of selling goldfish, Carina sold 36, and in the fifth week, she sold 45.) On the

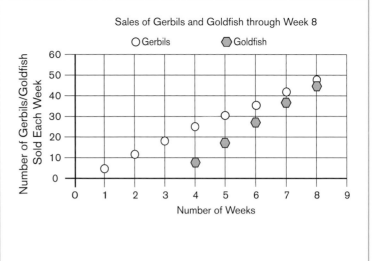

Week of Gerbil Sales	Number of Gerbil Sales	Week of Goldfish Sales	Number of Goldfish Sales
1	6	No goldfish were sold during the first three weeks that the store was opened.	
2	12		
3	18		
4	24	1	9
5	30	2	18
6	36	3	27
7	42	4	36
8	48	5	45
n	$6n$	$n - 3$	$9(n - 3)$

Fig. **11.**

A table and graph showing actual and projected weekly sales of gerbils and goldfish through week 8

basis of the patterns, the students should determine that by the end of week 8, Carina's sales of goldfish will come very close to her sales of gerbils (45 goldfish vs. 48 gerbils) but will not overtake them. What happens after week 8 is unknown!

Challenge your students to explain the algebraic expressions in the bottom row of the table in figure 11. Can they explain why the number of weeks for goldfish sales is $n - 3$? Or why the expression for number of goldfish sold each week is $9(n - 3)$? Can they analyze the slopes of the two linear relationships in the graph in terms of slope?

You can invent other scenarios for your students to explore with tables and graphs as well. An example follows:

> At the beginning of week 2, Carina added mice to her stock. Over the next three weeks, her mice sales increased at a constant rate of 4 each week. At the beginning of week 3, Carina added parakeets to her inventory, and her parakeet sales increased at a constant rate of 5 each week for the next 3 weeks. If Carina's weekly sales of these pets continue to increase at the same rates through week 8, will her weekly sales of parakeets overtake her weekly sales of mice before the end of week 8? If so, when?

Assessment

In this investigation, the students create tables and graphs to investigate rates of change. You can assess their understanding by having them work with other scenarios, or you can ask them to explain their tables and graphs and the relationships that they show. Pay close attention to the way that the students describe how a change in the dependent variable (*Number of animals sold each week*) relates to a change in the independent variable (*Number of weeks*).

Reflections

This investigation focuses on *rate of change* and *slope*, both important concepts in the study of algebra. Students should reflect on the

Week	Mice Sales	Parakeet Sales
1		
2	4	
3	8	5
4	12	10
5	16	15
6	20	20
7	24	25
8	28	30

By the end of week 6, sales of mice and parakeets will be equal (20 of each), and by the end of week 7, sales of parakeets will outpace sales of mice (25 sales of parakeets to 24 sales of mice).

relationship between independent and dependent variables and develop an understanding of how to represent the rate of change on a graph, using data from a table. After constructing the data table and graphing data points, they should think about the relationship between the x and y variables and write algebraic expressions to descibe the relationship between the number of weeks and the number of pets sold.

Connections

The students' work in this investigation draws on concepts and processes from data analysis and measurement. Students see the power of tables and graphs to help them measure quantities and discover relationships that they can then represent symbolically, building a solid foundation for an understanding of algebra.

Making and Breaking Solids

Focus

Reasoning about geometric relationships

Overview

This investigation helps students develop more sophisticated reasoning about decomposing and recomposing the interiors, or volumes, of three-dimensional shapes. Students improve their skills in visualizing spaces and broaden their understanding of volume, congruence, and geometric transformations. They also increase their ability to analyze shapes on the basis of their properties. The first task involves decomposing one three-dimensional shape to make another. The second task requires a comparison of two three-dimensional shapes to determine which has the greater volume. The third task focuses on decomposing a rectangular prism into congruent pieces. The fourth task calls for cutting a cube to make cross sections that are specified polygons. In each case, the students investigate possibilities by using either geoblocks or the 3-D Shape Decomposition Tool (on the CD-ROM).

Goals

- Improve reasoning about decomposing and recomposing shapes
- Develop skill in visualizing spatial possibilities
- Progress from approaching shapes by visualizing them to thinking about them analytically
- Think about congruence informally in applied situations

Mathematical Content

The ability to decompose two- and three-dimensional shapes carefully and analytically is an essential reasoning skill in mathematics. Students begin to develop this skill in the elementary grades, and they continue to use and refine it through and beyond calculus. Decomposing shapes allows students to find areas and volumes and understand fractional parts of regions. In addition, many advanced mathematical, scientific, and engineering applications use the decomposition of shapes in problem solving.

The ability to decompose two- and three-dimensional shapes carefully and analytically is an essential reasoning skill in mathematics.

Decomposing shapes gives students a strong foundation for reasoning about volume. Their work in this investigation helps them see that shapes that look different can have equal volume. Eventually, such ideas and experiences can lead students to an understanding of general methods for finding volumes of nonrectangular shapes. Students also think about other essential geometric concepts, such as *congruence, transformations,* and *properties of polygons.* The investigation directly or indirectly supports the following Geometry and Process Standards and expectations for grades 3–5 (NCTM 2000, pp. 396, 402):

Geometry

- Analyze characteristics and properties of two- and three-dimensional geometric shapes and develop mathematical arguments about geometric relationships
  - Identify, compare, and analyze attributes of two- and three-dimensional shapes and develop vocabulary to describe the attributes
  - Investigate, describe, and reason about the results of subdividing, combining, and transforming shapes
  - Explore congruence
  - Make and test conjectures about geometric properties and relationships and develop logical arguments to justify conclusions
- Apply transformations and use symmetry to analyze mathematical situations
  - Predict and describe the results of sliding, flipping, and turning two-dimensional shapes
- Use visualization, spatial reasoning, and geometric modeling to solve problems
  - Create and describe mental images of objects, patterns, and paths
  - Recognize geometric ideas and relationships and apply them to other disciplines and to problems that arise in the classroom or in everyday life

Problem Solving

- Build new mathematical knowledge through problem solving
- Solve problems that arise in mathematics and in other contexts

Reasoning and Proof

- Recognize reasoning and proof as fundamental aspects of mathematics

Students' Mathematical Thinking

Research has produced convincing evidence that an effective way to improve mathematics instruction and learning is for teachers to understand the mathematical thought processes of their students (Fennema et al. 1996). A research-based knowledge of students' construction of meaning for core mathematical ideas can enhance teachers' understanding. For decomposing and recomposing shapes, research has identified several basic levels of sophistication in reasoning (Battista 2001).

Level 1: Physical Decomposing and Recomposing

At this level, students have not sufficiently abstracted the images of shapes to visualize decomposing and recomposing shapes. They have great difficulty imagining how shapes can be decomposed, so they frequently imagine decomposition inaccurately. To be successful, they must decompose and recompose shapes physically, mainly through trial and error. As students make the transition to level 2 thinking, they start to visualize possible decompositions and recompositions but must test their ideas by using concrete materials.

Level 2: Visualized Decomposing and Recomposing

Students at this level have abstracted the images of shapes well enough that they can mentally envision decomposing and recomposing them without the use of concrete materials. Students might still draw pictures to help them think about decompositions, although drawing decompositions of three-dimensional shapes can be quite difficult.

Level 3: Visualized Decomposing and Recomposing with the Explicit Use of Measurement

At this level, students explicitly use measurements, in addition to visualization, to decompose and recompose shapes. They determine and compare areas by using measurement-guided decomposition. For instance, they use the lengths of sides to decide where to cut apart shapes and to decide if decomposed shapes are congruent.

Note: For most students and adults, reasoning about three-dimensional shapes depicted in drawings is considerably more difficult than reasoning about actual physical shapes. However, the ability to understand a three-dimensional shape depicted in a drawing is an important visual reasoning skill. The 3-D Shape Decomposition Tool on the CD-ROM can help students develop this skill because they can rotate the shapes on the computer screen. When users manipulate dynamic drawings of three-dimensional shapes on screen, their minds naturally interpret the shapes as three-dimensional.

Prior Knowledge or Experience

- Experience in analyzing two- and three-dimensional shapes by using pattern blocks or multilink cubes

- An informal introduction to concepts such as line, angle, symmetry, similarity, and congruence

Materials

For each student—
- A copy of each of the following blackline masters:
  - "Cutting and Making Solids"
  - "Geoblock Comparisons"
  - "Cutting a Rectangular Prism into Congruent Pieces"
  - "Cross Sections of a Cube"
- One or two colored pencils (different colors, if possible)

pp. 94–95; 96; 97–100; 101–102

For each pair of students—
- Access to the 3-D Shape Decomposition Tool (on the CD-ROM)

For the class—
- At least two complete sets of geoblocks (see fig. 12)

For the teacher—
- An overhead projector (optional)
- Transparencies of each of the following blackline masters (optional):

- ◦ "Cutting and Making Solids"
- ◦ "Geoblock Comparisons"
- ◦ "Cutting a Rectangular Prism into Congruent Pieces"
- ◦ "Cross Sections of a Cube"

Classroom Environment

Throughout this investigation, the students work in pairs, and students in each pair should be approximately equal in mathematical ability.

Investigation

Making and Breaking Solids consists of four tasks, each with its own activity sheet. At the beginning of each task, give each student a copy of the appropriate activity sheet. Pair the students, and tell them that they should discuss their thoughts with their partners as they work. However, emphasize that they should still record their own ideas on their own activity sheets.

To help your students progress to higher levels of thinking, each task involves them in the same process. First, they try to visualize the decomposition or recomposition necessary to solve a problem, then they make a conjecture, or "prediction," and finally they use physical materials or the 3-D Shape Decomposition Tool to check their proposed solutions. As your students work, ask questions that encourage them to visualize solutions instead of merely using physical trial and error. For each task, students should find, record, and check multiple possibilities.

As the students work on these tasks, they will use such geometric concepts as congruence and symmetry in naming and describing

Fig. 12.

A set of thirteen geoblocks

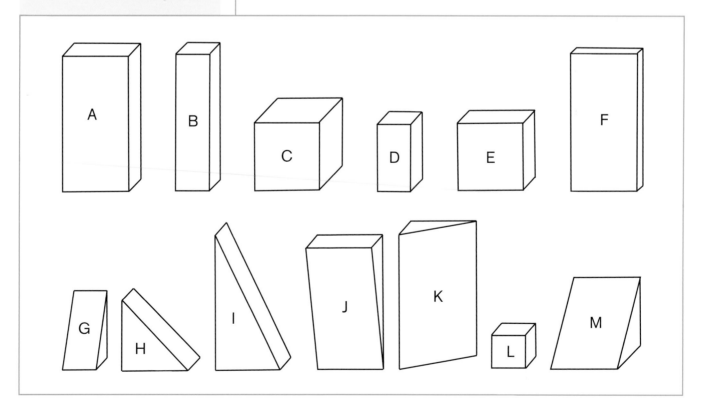

polygons. They should also use transformations—particularly, turns, or *rotations*. If your students use their own language to describe these concepts, you should introduce correct geometric terminology. For example, students might say "square corner" when they describe a *right angle*, or they might say that pieces are "identical" when they mean that the pieces are *congruent*.

Without saying that the informal terms that your students are using are wrong, have them clarify what they mean, and at the same time introduce correct terminology. For instance, you might ask, "How do I know what a 'square corner'—or *right angle*—looks like?" Students who do not yet understand the concept of angle measure or know what a 90-degree angle is might identify a right angle as the kind of angle that they find at the "corners" of a square or rectangle, such as a standard sheet of paper.

Walk around the classroom as the students work on a task. Observe their work, and occasionally ask them to explain or justify what they are doing. Ask them why some of their attempts at solutions fail and others succeed. Take note of how the students are making the decompositions or recompositions. Do they match up pieces of the solids according to side lengths or angle measures? Do they use properties of shapes to help them compare shapes? Record your observations of students' strategies so that you can use them both for assessment and as focal points in follow-up class discussions.

After each pair of students has completed the task, have all the pairs share their solutions, methods, and reasoning. You might record the students' solutions on overhead transparencies and then provide time for verifying different solutions. Encourage students to share a wide variety of ideas—even ones that were not successful. Also, have them explain how they found solutions and how their solutions satisfy the rules and special requirements of particular problems. Students' reflections on these questions will help them develop and enrich their concepts of symmetry and congruence.

Task 1—Cutting and Making Solids

Give each student a copy of the blackline master "Cutting and Making Solids," which shows six pairs of three-dimensional shapes. Assign each student a partner. For each pair of shapes, the students must identify a single "flat"—or *planar*—cut that they could make to shape 1 to "break," or "slice"—or *decompose*—it into two pieces that they could then recompose as shape 2. The students must describe the cut that they would make and draw line segments on shape 1 to show the cut and on shape 2 to show the joining of the resulting parts in the new shape.

Encourage the students to try out their descriptions of their cuts by stating them orally to their partners. If their partners understand the descriptions, the students will be ready to write them down on the activity sheet. Then they can draw line segments to show their cuts to shape 1 and their placement of the pieces in composing shape 2. This process will give the students opportunities to make important conceptual connections between two-dimensional drawings of three-dimensional shapes and the actual three-dimensional shapes.

It is important to note that some of the shapes drawn on the activity sheet will probably not look "right," because their proportions and

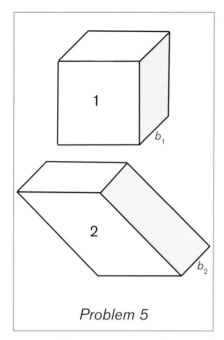

Problem 5

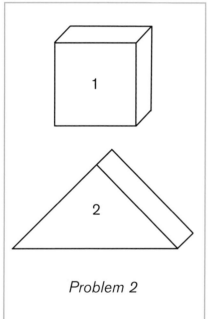

Problem 2

angles are not always what we are accustomed to expect in conventional "perspective" drawings of three-dimensional objects. The drawings on the activity sheet have no vanishing point. As drawn, the "backs" of the shapes are the same size as the "fronts," and there is no difference in scale between shape 1 and shape 2 to suggest that one is closer to the viewer than the other in space. (In other words, the drawings do not have a real foreground or background.)

Instead, the drawings meticulously preserve lengths, areas, and angles in all "front-facing," "top," or "side" views of the shapes. As a result, the students can make direct comparisons of lengths and of areas in all the "front-facing" views, all the "top" views, and all the "side" views.

Consider, for example, the "side" views in problem 5 (see the shapes in the margin, with the "side" views shaded). In these views, the segments that show the bases (b_1 and b_2) are equal. By the conventions of these drawings, this equality tells us to assume that these lengths are in fact the same. Consequently, since we interpret shape 1 as a cube, we are to conclude that b_2, the base that we see on the side of shape 2, actually has the same measure as an *edge of the cube* in shape 1.

This way of "reading" the drawing is not how we would ordinarily "see" such a drawing. In fact, standard drawing conventions would make us much more likely to "see" shape 2 in problem 5 as a different view of the block that appears as shape 1 in problem 2 (see the margin). We might easily suppose that a "half-cube" block such as that pictured in problem 2 has simply been pulled to the foreground and tipped slightly in problem 5.

Help your students see that the shapes have been drawn in such a way that they can slice shape 1 into two solids that they can imagine putting together to make shape 2 *exactly as drawn on the page*. The activity sheet carries an explanatory note about the drawings, but the ideas may be difficult for students to understand, and you may need to amplify or clarify them.

After the students have finished the problems on the sheet, they should check their work by using either the 3-D Shape Decomposition Tool or geoblocks (see fig. 12; have at least two complete sets available in the classroom). If the students use the electronic decomposition tool, they will need to manipulate the images on the screen, often "turning" them to understand what shapes they represent. If they are working with geoblocks, they must accommodate the fact that they cannot actually slice the blocks. To simulate slicing a block, they should find two blocks that they can put together to replicate shape 1 with a cut like the one that they drew on the activity sheet. Then they must rearrange the two blocks to make shape 2, thus confirming their work on the problem.

For example, to verify their solution to problem 1, the students can find two blocks of the type labeled "E" in figure 12, stack them to make shape 1 with a cut-line showing, and then rearrange the two blocks to make shape 2 (see fig. 13). Likewise, the students can use two blocks of the type labeled "H" to check their work on problem 2, two blocks of type M to check problem 3, two blocks of type K to check problem 4, two blocks of type M to check problem 5, and two blocks of type J to check problem 6.

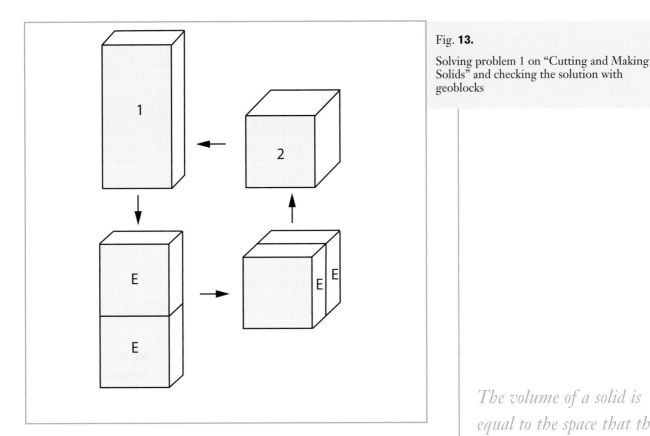

Task 2—Geoblock Comparisons

The second task should not present the students with a great deal of difficulty after their work on the first task. Give each student a copy of the blackline master "Geoblock Comparisons." Have the students continue to work with their partners, and keep the geoblocks out in the classroom.

The activity sheet includes the drawing shown in figure 12 of a set of thirteen geoblocks. The students examine eight pairs of these blocks, identified by their letter labels. For each pair, the students must decide which block has the greater volume or whether the volumes of the two blocks are equal.

Remind the students, "The volume of a solid is the amount of space it occupies." Say, "Look carefully at each pair of blocks. Is the volume of one block greater than the volume of the other block, or do the two blocks have the same volume?" Tell the students to think of their answers as predictions, which may or may not turn out to be true when the students check them by using actual blocks.

The drawings on the activity sheet "Geoblock Comparisons," like those on "Cutting and Making Solids," are not completely conventional in their representation of three dimensions in two-dimensional space. Consider, for example, the drawings of blocks G and H (see the margin). If we assumed that these drawings used standard techniques of foreshortening, we might well "see" the shape labeled "H" simply as another view of block G, now turned with its side facing us.

However, by the different conventions of these drawings, block G represents one-half of block D, and block H represents one-half of block E. (Block G is produced by slicing D from one top edge through the opposite bottom edge; block H is produced by slicing block E from

The volume of a solid is equal to the space that the solid occupies.

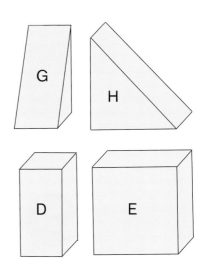

one of its shorter top edges through its opposite bottom edge.) As before, a note on the activity sheet attempts to explain the drawings, but students may find the ideas difficult to grasp.

Once the students understand how to interpret lengths, areas, and angles in the drawings, help them reason about the problems on the activity page by asking a variety of questions. For instance, if the students have difficulty with problem 1, which calls on them to compare the volumes of blocks A and B, ask, "If you had more than one block that was just like block B, could you use these blocks to duplicate block A?" If the students agree, follow up by asking, "How many blocks like block B would you need?"

The students should conclude that they would need just two blocks like block B for this task (see fig. 14). Then ask them, "What does this fact tell you about the volumes of blocks A and B? How are these volumes related?" They should see that block B is half of block A, so the volume of block B is half the volume of block A.

Problem 4 asks students to compare the volumes of blocks B and F. If students are having difficulty with this problem, you might guide them in a little transitive reasoning. Ask, "How many blocks like block B did you need in problem 1 to make block A?" (2) Next, ask, "How many blocks like block F would you need to make block A?" They should see that they would also need two blocks for this task. On the board, make a drawing like that in figure 15 to illustrate the situation. Say, "One block B plus another block B makes block A, which we can also make another way, with one block F plus block F." Ask, "What does this tell you about the volumes of blocks B and F? How are they related?"

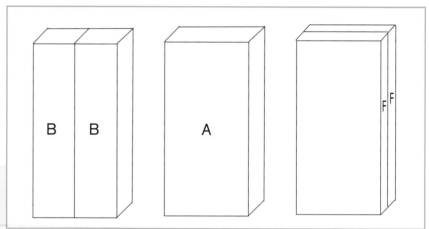

Fig. **15.**

Visualizing problem 4 on "Geoblock Comparisons"

Fig. **14.**

Visualizing problem 1 on "Geoblock Comparisons"

See if your students can reason that block B is thus one-half of block A, and block F is also one-half of block A. So block B and block F have the same volume. Explain, if necessary; this sort of reasoning, as logical as it seems to adults, can be very difficult for fifth graders. But transitive reasoning is essential to the study of mathematics, so teachers should take every opportunity to help students develop it.

Task 3—Cutting a Rectangular Prism into Congruent Pieces

The students should now be ready for the third task. Give each student a copy of the blackline master "Cutting a Rectangular Prism into Congruent Pieces." Have the students continue to work in pairs, and give each pair access to the 3-D Shape Decomposition Tool.

Navigating through Problem Solving and Reasoning in Grade 5

Problem 1(*a*) presents a drawing of a rectangular prism (see the margin). On the drawing, dots mark off equal line segments on the prism's edges. The students must identify a planar cut that would slice through the prism at marked dots to produce two congruent parts. Restricting the cuts to those that pass through dots limits the possibilities to a manageable, finite number. Otherwise, there would be an infinite number of ways of slicing the prism into two congruent parts. Figure 16 shows three possible cuts.

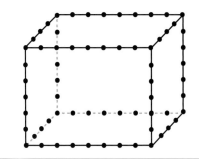

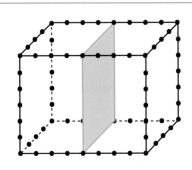 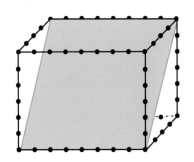 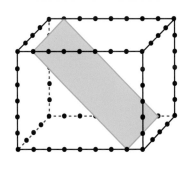

Fig. **16.**

Three planar cuts that pass through dots and divide the rectangular prism into two congruent solids

Problem 1(*b*) asks the students find other planar cuts that they could use to decompose the rectangular prism into two congruent parts. Have the students record their cuts by drawing segments on the faces of the prism and shading the cross section made by their cut. (Let the students use a colored pencil for the shading.) Then have them check their answers by using the 3-D Shape Decomposition Tool.

As the students propose solutions to parts *a* and *b* of problem 1, ask, "Why do you think the parts are congruent? Is there anything in your sketch that makes you certain?" (Students can use the evenly spaced dots to verify that corresponding side lengths are the same.) These types of questions can help students connect their identification of congruent parts to measurement and thus can move their thinking toward level 3.

A cut may make congruent parts that are actually the same as those made by a "mirror image" cut that "slants" the opposite way (see fig. 17). Encourage your students to think of any such pair of cuts as giving them the same solution, since they can rotate the pieces from the two cuts and see that they are the same. Urge your students to try to identify only unique solutions. The Solutions section shows eighteen unique ways to slice the rectangular prism into two congruent parts. Let your students check their work with the 3-D Shape Decomposition Tool.

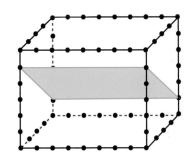 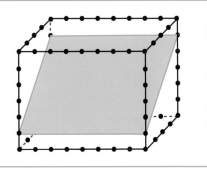

Fig. **17.**

"Mirror-image" cuts that produce identical solutions to problem 2

In problem 2(*a*), the students determine whether they can decompose the rectangular prism into three or four congruent parts by using two flat cuts. Have them record their cuts by drawing segments on the faces of the prism and shading the cross sections as before. (You can have the students shade the cross sections in different colors if they have pencils in more than one color.)

The students search for other solutions in 2(*b*). Then they should again check their answers by using the 3-D Shape Decomposition Tool. Figure 18a shows two cuts that slice through dots to divide the rectangular prism into three congruent parts, and figure 18b shows two pairs of cuts that divide the prism into four congruent parts.

There is only one way to use two cuts through dots to slice the prism into three congruent parts. The dots on the vertical edges of the prism divide each edge into six sections. Because 6 is evenly divisible by 3, the students can make two parallel cuts that pass through these edges and divide the prism into three congruent parts. The dots divide the other edges into either eight or four segments. Because neither 8 nor 4 is divisible by 3, the students cannot make two cuts that slice through dots on these edges to divide the prism into three congruent parts.

The Solutions section shows eighteen unique ways to make two planar cuts through dots to divide the rectangular prism into four congruent parts. Note that each solution shows a solution from problem 1 with a second cut that splits both of those congruent parts.

As your students work, have them describe or name the polygons formed by the cross sections that their cuts make. Ask, "Which of these polygons are congruent?"

Task 4—Cross Sections of a Cube

Building seamlessly on the third task, the fourth task focuses on possible shapes of cross sections of a cube. Give a copy of the blackline master "Cross Sections of a Cube" to each student. Again have the students work in pairs, with access to the 3-D Shape Decomposition Tool.

The students now must find flat cuts that will slice a cube in such a way that the cross sections make the following polygons:

- a square
- a rectangle that is not a square
- a triangle that is not equilateral
- a trapezoid
- an equilateral triangle

Fig. **18.**

Using two planar cuts, as in problem 2, to produce (a) three congruent parts or (b) four congruent parts

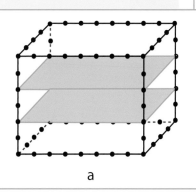

a

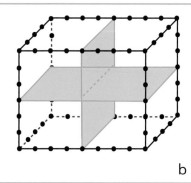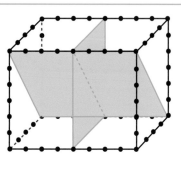

b

Navigating through Problem Solving and Reasoning in Grade 5

Again the students should record their solutions by drawing line segments on the faces of the cube and shading the resulting cross section with a colored pencil. They should then check their solutions by working with the 3-D Shape Decomposition Tool.

As your students succeed in slicing the cube in a way that produces a particular polygon, have them explain their work and the result. You might ask, "What makes that shape a square?" After the student conveys the idea that a square has four equal sides and four right angles, ask, "How do you know that all the sides of your shape are equal and that all of its angles are right angles?" Such questions can help students connect three-dimensional decompositions to properties of polygons, thus moving their ideas toward level 3 thinking. Also, for each polygon on the list, ask the students, "Is there more than one way to cut the cube to get a cross section in this shape?" When the students say yes, have them show different ways.

Figure 19 shows one solution for each shape on the list. Multiple solutions exist for each type of shape.

Assessment

As your students work, make ongoing assessments of their developing strategies and reasoning. Evaluate the students' performance during small-group work, and examine their individual work on the worksheets.

As your students work with their partners, listen carefully to their conversations to gather information about their reasoning and strategies. Ask questions to help you understand their thinking. Relate this information to the levels of reasoning about decomposition and recomposition described at the beginning of this investigation.

For instance, try to ascertain whether students are using concrete materials, making drawings, or simply visualizing the shapes to determine solutions. Try to observe whether students are using length (perhaps by counting segments between dots) to determine whether shapes that look the same on paper would actually be the same in three-dimensional space.

Reflections

The experiences in visualizing three-dimensional shapes that this investigation offers students will help them decompose and recompose shapes mentally. The investigation encourages the use of visualization in connection with analytic reasoning about shapes. The students should begin to see that their skills in visualizing shapes can support

Fig. 19.

Sample solutions to "Cross Sections of Solids"

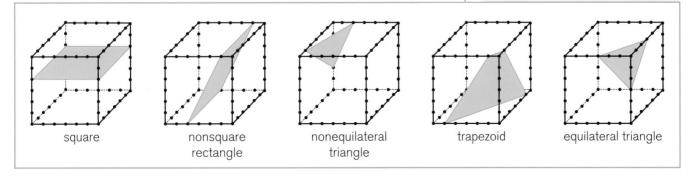

| square | nonsquare rectangle | nonequilateral triangle | trapezoid | equilateral triangle |

their reasoning as they compare sides, angles, and faces—often using measurements as they work.

As students encounter other tasks like those in the investigation, their abilities to visualize and reason about shapes will continue to grow. By integrating these skills with their expanding knowledge of length, angle measures, properties of shapes, and other geometric concepts, they will become more proficient in their visual analysis of shapes. For instance, students will eventually be able to explain why shapes are congruent by attending to the lengths of their sides. The dots that tasks 3 and 4 show on the edges of the rectangular prisms invite students to compare the measures of the sides. Such comparisons can help them decide whether two shapes are congruent or how they might fit together.

The geometry investigations in *Navigating through Problem Solving and Reasoning in Grade 3* (Yeatts et al. 2004) and *Navigating through Problem Solving and Reasoning in Grade 4* (Yeatts et al. 2005) also focus on decomposing and recomposing shapes to develop similar reasoning skills but in the simpler context of two-dimensional shapes. These units can serve as resources to support your students' work on three-dimensional composition.

Connections

Your students' work in this investigation can buttress their understanding of and facility in measuring volume. Specifically, students need to develop their skills in the spatial structuring of three-dimensional arrays—a concept necessary for a genuine understanding of volume (Battista 1998, 1999, 2002; Battista and Berle-Carman 1996).

Comparing Ourselves with Others

Focus

Reasoning about measurement relationships

Overview

Students have many experiences with measurement in the elementary grades, with both standard units of measure and nonstandard units. They frequently measure lengths, find areas of such familiar shapes as rectangles and triangles, and weigh common objects. However, can we truly say that students have developed or are developing *measurement sense*? Do they genuinely think about the measurements that they make and consider their reasonableness? Do they relate measurements in mathematics lessons to measurements that they discover in other contexts? Elementary students too often skim over measurements that they encounter in their reading, without stopping to think about what these

really mean. If students read that a hummingbird weighs about $\frac{1}{30}$ of

an ounce, for example, do they try to come up with a benchmark to make the measurement meaningful? A hummingbird weighs less than a dime. The amazing lightness of the hummingbird comes into focus when students compare its weight with that of some known quantity. This investigation helps fifth graders make such comparisons.

Fifth grade marks the transition from elementary school to middle school, and this is the year when students begin to convert from one unit to another. They work with derived units, such as miles per hour, and start to consider the idea of proportion in measurement. In this investigation, students encounter these concepts as they compare measurements of themselves with measurements of animals, other people (including an imaginary giant), and various objects.

Goals

- Compare measurements of different attributes of the same object (or animal or person) or measurements of the same attribute in different objects (or animals or persons)
- Convert from one unit of measure to another
- Evaluate the reasonableness of statements about measurements

Mathematical Content

This investigation supports the following Measurement and Process Standards and expectations for grades 3–5 (NCTM 2000, pp. 398, 402):

Measurement
- Understand measurable attributes of objects and the units, systems, and processes of measurement

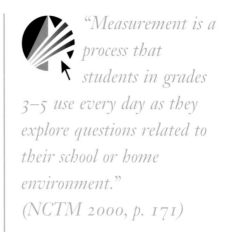

"Measurement is a process that students in grades 3–5 use every day as they explore questions related to their school or home environment."
(NCTM 2000, p. 171)

Encourage your students to reflect on the measurements that they encounter in books or newspapers or on television, comparing these measurements to known benchmarks.

- Understand such attributes as length, area, weight, [and] volume... and select the appropriate type of unit for measuring each attribute
- Carry out simple unit conversions ... within a system of measurement
- Explore what happens to measurements of a two-dimensional shape such as its perimeter and area when the shape is changed in some way

- Apply appropriate techniques, tools, and formulas to determine measurements
  - Develop strategies for estimating the perimeters, areas, and volumes of irregular shapes
  - Select and apply appropriate standard units and tools to measure length, area, volume, [and] weight

Problem Solving

- Solve problems that arise in mathematics and in other contexts
- Apply and adapt a variety of appropriate strategies to solve problems

Reasoning and Proof

- Select and use various types of reasoning and methods of proof

In this investigation, students use measurements of such attributes as weight, height, area, and speed to make comparisons between themselves and various animals, people, and objects. As part of their study of speed, students begin work with derived units—a topic that they will study in greater depth in the middle grades—and they estimate a given distance and compare their estimate with the actual measure of that distance. A task in which the students compare their own measurements with those of an imaginary giant provides an informal introduction to another topic that students will study formally in the middle grades—proportional reasoning.

The students use problem-solving strategies throughout the investigation as they relate measurement and numerical skills. For instance, they determine how long it takes them to walk or jog one hundred feet, and they use this measurement to find how long it takes them to walk or jog one mile. By working with this result, the students can determine their walking or running speed, in either minutes per mile or miles per minute. The students can solve all the problems in the investigation in more than one way, depending on their skills.

Prior Knowledge or Experience

- Experience in using a ruler to measure length
- Experience in using a stopwatch, a wristwatch with a second hand, or some other device for measuring time in seconds
- An understanding of the concepts of area and volume
- An understanding of the operations of multiplication and division
- Experience in making computations with a calculator (either four-function or scientific)

- Experience in using reference books or the Internet to find information

Materials

For each student—

- A copy of each of the following blackline masters:
  - "Measuring Up with Animals"
  - "A Snail's Pace"
  - "Time to Walk vs. Time to Jog"
  - "Faster than a Speeding Ostrich?"
  - "Is There a Giant in the House?"
- Four sheets of inch grid paper (template available as a blackline master)
- A sheet of half-inch grid paper (optional; template available on the CD-ROM)
- A sheet of quarter-inch grid paper (optional; template available on the CD-ROM)

For each group of four or five students—

- A length of string (optional; about 36 inches)
- A copy of the blackline master "Walking and Jogging Times"
- A calculator (either four-function or scientific)
- Rulers, yardsticks (or metersticks), or measuring tapes
- A stopwatch (or a wristwatch or clock with a second hand)

For the classroom—

- Reference books or access to the Internet for locating information about animals
- Several rolls of transparent tape
- Several pairs of scissors
- Everyday objects, such as a comb, brush, toothbrush, fork, or spoon

For the teacher—

- Four sheets of one-inch grid paper (template available as a blackline master), trimmed and taped together to form one large sheet (length and width in the about same ratio as in a single small sheet)
- A copy of the each of the following children's books
  - *Biggest, Strongest, Fastest* (Jenkins 1995)
  - *What's Faster than a Speeding Cheetah?* (Wells 1997)
  - *Jim and the Beanstalk* (Briggs 1970) or *Gulliver in Lilliput* (Hodges 1995)

Classroom Environment

Students work individually, in pairs, or in small groups in different parts of the investigation, depending on the task and the teacher's

pp. 103–105; 106; 107; 108; 109; 110–11; 112–15

If the children's books suggested in the materials list are not available, many other titles can serve as suitable substitutes. For ideas, see the children's literature section in the references to this book, especially Thiessen (2004) and Whiten and Whiten (2004).

preferences. Small groups will be most effective in the second part of task 2, where the students estimate and measure a hundred feet and determine how quickly they can walk or jog that distance. In task 3, where each student needs a classmate's help to measure various physical attributes, girls will probably be more comfortable in working with girls, and boys, with boys. Before the students begin task 3, the whole class should discuss the concept of determining a ratio to use to find the dimensions of giant-sized attributes and objects.

Investigation

The investigation Comparing Ourselves with Others consists of three tasks, each with its own activity sheet(s) and focusing on different types of comparison. Three children's books serve as springboards to the activities. (If the specified books are not available, you can substitute others with the same themes.)

Task 1—Measuring Up with Animals

To introduce the first task, read aloud to the class the children's picture book *Biggest, Strongest, Fastest* (Jenkins 1995). This book identifies fourteen different animals that hold "world records" for particular attributes or skills (for example, the Etruscan shrew is the world's smallest mammal; it is small enough to sleep curled in a teaspoon).

Before turning a page to reveal a pictured animal, have the students predict which animal holds the next "world record." For example, before showing the picture of the African elephant, ask, "What animal do you suppose holds the title of biggest land animal?" Students will probably suggest the elephant. Then show the illustration of the African elephant. Reading the book in this way will not only keep the students focused but also provide connections to science by highlighting characteristics of animals that the students have studied throughout elementary school.

Your students are likely to find the information in *Biggest, Strongest, Fastest* engaging, but you will probably observe that many of them do not really think about the meanings or magnitudes of the measurements. Give each student a copy of the blackline master "Measuring Up with Animals," which asks questions designed to make the students think very concretely by comparing measurements of the animals with measurements of themselves or a typical fifth grader.

Note that in the activity students need not weigh themselves or measure their own heights. Because students sometimes make comparisons of their own weights or heights that are painful to some individuals, the activity sheet provides average weights and heights for a ten-year-old boy and a ten-year-old girl in the United States. Your students can use these average measurements instead of their own. Alternatively, you can ask for a student to volunteer his or her weight and height for all the students to use in their computations.

Make sure that your students have access to a calculator. The students' attention should be on a measurement and its connection with some benchmark related to a personal measurement rather than on cumbersome pencil-and-paper computations.

Colorful cut-paper collages present fourteen "record-holding" animals in *Biggest, Strongest, Fastest* (Jenkins 1995). Although the book targets children aged 4–9, facts in smaller type add interest for older children – and adults. These extra facts bring in concepts of scale and proportion, and small silhouettes show relative sizes. A chart at the back of the book provides additional information on such topics as the animals' diets and habitats.

Hendrix-Martin (1997) and Oleson (1998) both present "amazing comparison" activities that are similar to those in task 1. Hendrix-Martin's activities use *Biggest, Strongest, Fastest* (Jenkins 1995); Oleson focuses on data collection. Both authors' work is available on the CD-ROM.

Each question on the activity sheet calls for a comparison based on measurements. For instance, the students must consider the fact that an elephant eats about three hundred pounds of grass in a day. Then they compare this weight with their own weight (or that of a typical ten-year-old). This comparison gives the students a new perspective on the elephant's daily consumption of grass. Students are usually amazed to realize that an elephant eats the equivalent in weight of three or four fifth graders a day!

Later, the activity sheet directs the students to compare the area covered by their hand with the area covered by the body and legs of a South American bird spider. This spider's leg span—just slightly more than eleven inches—makes it the largest spider in the world. To show your students approximately how large an area the leg span covers, draw a circle with an eleven-inch diameter on one-inch grid paper.

Unfortunately, such a circle is too large to fit on a single standard sheet of grid paper. Otherwise, drawing the circle would be a very good exercise for the students. To construct a circle with an eleven-inch diameter for your students to inspect, print four sheets of one-inch grid paper from the template in this book, trim them as necessary, align gridlines, and tape grids together to create a single grid large enough to accommodate the circle. Display your finished work on a wall or bulletin board where the students can come up individually, in pairs, or in small groups to count squares in the grid to approximate the area of the circle. Be sure to remind the students that the area covered by the bird spider would not be perfectly circular. Explain that a circle nevertheless gives a useful representation of the area occupied by the spider.

Give each student a sheet of one-inch grid paper (also printed from the template in the book), and have the students trace a hand as directed on the activity sheet (fingers closed up to one another, and thumb closed up to the side of the hand). Again they will count squares to estimate the area. The students then compare this area to that of the circle with an eleven-inch diameter.

As the students make their comparisons of the two areas (question 3[*c*] on the activity page), many are likely to use additive reasoning. That is, they may make a comparison based on the *difference* between the two areas, rather than a comparison based on their *ratio*, as the question requires. To encourage the students to think multiplicatively, emphasize that the question asks them to tell how many hand-areas they would need to make an area equal to that covered by the bird spider. Thinking correctly about this question will help lay a foundation for proportional reasoning and will prepare the students for the third task in the investigation—Is There a Giant in the House?

To extend the activity to include the idea of increasing the precision of a measurement, you might have each student make outlines of his or her hand on several sheets of grid paper, each with a different-sized grid. The CD-ROM includes the templates "Half-Inch Grid Paper" and "Quarter-Inch Grid Paper" for this purpose. Discuss with the class the relationship between the size of the unit and the precision that is possible in the resulting measurement. Be sure that the students understand that the smaller the unit, the more precise a measurement can be.

As another extension, you might let the students use a length of string (about 36 inches) to find the perimeter of their hand and the

Use the template "One-Inch Grid Paper" (in the book and on the CD-ROM) to print four sheets of grid paper that you can tape together to accommodate a circle with a diameter of eleven inches. Print enough additional sheets of one-inch grid paper to give a sheet to each student to use in tracing a hand.

You can print grid paper with different-sized grids from the templates "Half-Inch Grid Paper" and "Quarter-Inch Grid Paper" available on the CD-ROM.

In addition to *Biggest, Strongest, Fastest* (Jenkins 1995), other titles that students can use to find record holders include *Incredible Comparisons* (Ash 1996), *Highest, Longest, Deepest: A Fold-Out Guide to the World's Record Breakers* (Malam 1996), *How Big Were the Dinosaurs?* (Most 1994), and *If You Hopped Like a Frog* (Schwartz 1999).

Making a scale drawing helps students put comparisons into perspective.

circumference of the circle representing the bird spider's leg span. Then they can compare these lengths, again making a comparison based on multiplicative rather than additive reasoning. Remove your circle from the wall or bulletin board and place it flat on a table for this exercise.

To conclude task 1, the students identify a record-holding animal that they haven't considered so far (or a record-making phenomenon that is inanimate, such as the highest mountain in the world). They compare their own skill or size to the record-making quality of this new animal (or other phenomenon). The students should look for record-holders in a book or on the Internet. Be sure to have several resources available so that the students can make a comparison that interests them (see the upper left margin for several possibilities).

One fifth-grader discovered that a sun jellyfish has poisonous tentacles that can extend 200 feet (2400 inches) in the water. This student compared the reach of the jellyfish with her own height—61 inches.

She found that the jellyfish was $\frac{2400}{61}$, or approximately 39, times her height. When asked to make a scale drawing by using one inch to represent her own height and showing her height and the reach of the jellyfish in an accurate ratio, she taped standard sheets of paper together end to end until she had a strip long enough to make the scale drawing.

Another student compared herself with a giant sequoia tree, which often grows to about 300 feet. This student was about 4 feet tall, making the tree 75 times her height. After taping together sheets of paper, she made a scale drawing that showed her height as one inch and height of the tree as 75 inches, and then she and her teacher taped the drawing to the ceiling of the school cafeteria.

Task 2—Getting from Here to There

The second task involves comparisons related to *speed*. The task has three parts. The first part, "A Snail's Pace," introduces students to the idea of speed as they compare their own time over a given distance to the time that a snail would take to traverse the same distance. The second part, "Time to Walk vs. Time to Jog," reinforces the idea that speed is a derived measurement that relates measurements of time and distance multiplicatively. The third part, "Faster than a Speeding Ostrich?" gives the students a new opportunity to apply this idea as they compare their own times to travel a particular distance to the times that particular animals or motorized vehicles would take.

Introduce Getting from Here to There by saying, "How long does it take you to travel from one place to another?" Be sure that the students understand that they need two pieces of information to answer this question: how far one place is from the other and how fast they are traveling. The three parts of the activity, all with blackline masters, will give them opportunities to compare the time that it would take them to get from one place to another with the time that it would take a given animal, other people, or someone in a motorized vehicle.

Navigating through Problem Solving and Reasoning in Grade 5

Part 1—A Snail's Pace. Again show the students the picture of the land snail in the book *Biggest, Strongest, Fastest* (Jenkins 1995). The land snail is a very slow animal, traveling only about eight inches in one minute. In the first part of task 2, the students use this fact to reason about the time that a snail would need to traverse other distances. To begin, have each student estimate the distance, in inches, from the left edge to the right edge of his or her desk. Then have each student estimate the time the snail would need to cross the desk.

Give each student a copy of the blackline master "A Snail's Pace." This activity sheet directs them to measure their desks from edge to edge. After the students have made their measurements, have them compare these with their estimates. This exercise will give them a new benchmark for future work with length. Next, the activity sheet asks the students to calculate the time the snail would need to cross the desk.

You may decide to have your students work in pairs or groups to complete the next step—measuring the distance from the classroom to the cafeteria (or another, more convenient location in the school). Give them a yardstick or a measuring tape and have them measure in feet. For the next step—finding how long they take to walk this distance at their usual pace, give them a stopwatch or be sure that they have a wristwatch with a second hand. Emphasize that this activity is not a race. The students should walk the distance at a normal pace—no faster, as many undoubtedly will try to do.

Next, the students must find the time that a snail would take to travel the same distance. Because the snail takes one minute to traverse eight inches, the students should see that the number of eight-inch segments in the distance is theoretically equal to the number of minutes that the snail would take to traverse it. However, your students might come up with a variety of strategies that seem easier to them than multiplying the number of feet by 12 to convert to inches and dividing the product by 8 to determine how many eight-inch segments the distance contains.

In one class, for example, some students constructed an eight-inch segment by snapping together multilink cubes. They then used this tool to measure the distance from their classroom to the cafeteria in eight-inch segments, marking off each segment lightly in pencil as they worked. Then they counted the segments and assigned one minute to each to find how many minutes the snail would take to travel the distance. Other students observed that there are 4.5 eight-inch segments in a yardstick (36 inches ÷ 8 inches = 4.5). They then determined the number of "yardsticks" (yards) contained in the distance and multiplied that number by 4.5 to find the number of 8-inch segments.

The last question on "A Snail's Pace" asks the students, "How many times faster than the snail were you?" When your students are comparing their times with the time it would take the snail to travel the distance between the classroom and the cafeteria, again be sure that they are using multiplicative rather than additive reasoning. Remind them that the question isn't asking, "*How much longer* would the snail take to travel the distance than you took?" This comparison question would ask for the *difference* between the student's time and the snail's. Show the students that they could express this *additive* relationship as "*Snail's time* + □ = *My time*," or "*My time* − *Snail's time* = □."

To build their measurement sense, students need to estimate measurements before actually making them.

Many sites on the Internet provide fascinating information on record-holding animals and other natural phenomena. The following represent only a small sample:

- http://nationalzoo.si.edu/ Animals/AnimalRecords

- http://www.4to40.com/ recordbook/default .asp?category=animal

- http://www.extremescience .com/record_index.htm

- http://oceanlink.island.net/ records.html

- http://ufbir.ifas.ufl.edu

By contrast, the question on the activity sheet asks, "*How many times faster* than the snail were you?" See if your students can understand that instead of asking them about the difference between a student's time and the snail's, this question asks for the *quotient* of the student's time divided by the snail's. They can express this *multiplicative* relationship as "*Snail's time* × □ = *My time*," or "*My time* ÷ *Snail's time* = □."

Part 2—Time to Walk vs. Time to Jog. In the second part of Getting from Here to There, the students go first to the playground (or physical education area) to collect data on their walking and jogging times. They return to the classroom to estimate their times for other distances before collecting information at home on the distance to school. Finally, back in the classroom again, they complete their computations and discuss their work.

Give each student a copy of the blackline master "Time to Walk vs. Time to Jog." Divide the students into groups of four or five, and let each group have a single copy of the related blackline master "Walking and Jogging Times." This second activity sheet shows a table for each group to complete together. (Making only one table will greatly simplify paperwork for the students.) Be sure that each group also has two yardsticks (or a measuring tape) and a stopwatch (or a wristwatch with a second hand).

Explain that the first activity sheet (which each student has) lists all the steps in the activity. Have the students in each group gather the materials listed in step 1, and send them to the playground (or the physical education area) to begin work. If you send your students to an outdoor area, be sure that it offers a level 100-foot course that they can measure.

Step 2 directs the students to estimate a distance of 100 feet over level terrain. Students often have difficulty in estimating distances of this magnitude; they typically have had little experience in making such estimates. Estimating a distance, marking off the estimate, making an actual measurement, and comparing the estimate and the measurement are important steps in developing measurement fluency. This process also helps students establish benchmarks that are important for future estimates of other distances.

After a group has made its estimate, the students need to measure the distance and adjust it to mark out a course of 100 feet. Have the students use their group's two yardsticks to "leap-frog" each other as they measure this distance. Note that students may pick up both yardsticks at the same time, thus "losing their place" in the measurement. Help students think about how to use the two yardsticks together to make the measurement.

When the students have marked off 100 feet, have them walk or jog this distance and record their time. Encourage them to walk or jog at a pace they could keep up for an extended period of time.

Next, the students return to the classroom and work with these times for 100 feet to determine theoretical times for a mile. Discuss with the students the fact that a mile equals 5280 feet. Ask the students, "How many groups of 100 feet are there in 5280?" The students should understand that there are 52.8 groups of 100 feet in one mile. So the students would multiply the time it takes them to walk or jog 100 feet by 52.8 to find the time that it takes them to walk or jog one mile.

Another strategy that students might use to compute time for a mile is to divide the time it takes them to walk or jog 100 feet by 100 to find the time it takes them to walk or jog one foot (a time that would be very difficult to measure directly). They would then multiply the result by 5280 (the number of feet in a mile).

The next step is to have the students determine the distance from home to school. Assign this step as homework. Working with a family member can help the students make a home-school connection in mathematics. When the students have brought their data back to the classroom, let them work with their times for walking and jogging a mile to find their times for walking and jogging from home to school. Calculators will make this job relatively simple. Moreover, many elementary students live less than a mile from school, so this work can give them opportunities to use decimals.

When every group has completed the table on the blackline master "Walking and Jogging Times," engage the whole class in a discussion of the work. A good point to consider is whether the students walked or jogged at a pace that they could maintain over a distance as long as a mile. Since this is almost certainly not the case, their computed values for walking and jogging a mile are likely to be *underestimates* of the actual time—perhaps by a wide margin.

Your students might find it interesting to compare their own jogging times for a mile with those of runners in a major marathon (26.2 miles), such as the Boston or New York City marathon, or with the times of shorter-distance Olympic runners in, say, a 100-meter race (≈ 328 ft). The students could discuss why speeds for shorter distances are so much greater than speeds for longer distances.

Part 3—Faster than a Speeding Ostrich? To introduce the third part of Getting from Here to There, read aloud to the class the children's book *What's Faster than a Speeding Cheetah?* (Wells 1997), which compares the speeds of various phenomena—animals, airplanes, rockets, meteors, and light. When you have finished reading the book, give each student a copy of the blackline master "Faster than a Speeding Ostrich?" Let the students work by themselves or in pairs on the sheet.

In this part of task 2, the students find the distance from their city to a favorite place in their region (a national park, theme park, amusement park, zoo, or some other public place). They then check back in their work in the previous part of task 2 and use their time to jog a mile to compute the time that they would take to reach their selected place on foot. Next, they compute the times that an ostrich, a cheetah, a peregrine falcon, a small plane, and a jet would take to travel the same distance (fig. 20 shows the table, based on data in Wells's book, which the students complete on the activity sheet). All the times are theoretical, of course, since each assumes that the student, animal, or motorized vehicle is capable of maintaining a steady pace for a very long time.

Interesting discussions have developed in classrooms where students have worked on the activity. One teacher observed a group of students determining how long it would take a peregrine falcon to travel 90 miles to the selected location at the speed given for the bird—200 miles per hour. Using a calculator, the students correctly divided 90 by 200 and got 0.45. Initially, however, they were perplexed about what 0.45 represented. Some suggested that the unit was minutes; others decided

Animal or Motorized Vehicle	Speed (miles per hour)	Time Needed to Travel to My Place (hours)
You		
Ostrich	45	
Cheetah	70	
Peregrine falcon	200	
Small plane	300	
Jet plane	600	

that it must be seconds, since the falcon's time had to be less than that of the cheetah, which they had already determined would travel the 90 miles in 1.3 hours.

The students finally realized that the correct unit for 0.45 was hours, but they then struggled to figure out how many minutes 0.45 hours would equal. Some students suggested subtracting 45 minutes from 60 minutes, getting 15 minutes. Others recognized that $\frac{1}{2}$ hr = 0.5 hr = 30 minutes, and they rounded 0.45 to 0.5, thus deciding that the time would be close to 30 minutes. In fact, the actual answer is 3 minutes less:

$$0.45 \times 60 = \frac{45}{100} \times 60 = \frac{9}{2} \times 6 = 9 \times 3 = 27$$

The teacher continued to observe as the students divided 90 miles by 300 miles per hour to determine the time for a small plane to travel to the selected place. Using a calculator, the students computed the time as 0.3 hr, recognizing the unit more confidently this time. To determine how many minutes 0.3 hours would be, the students considered a fact that they knew—that $\frac{1}{10}$ of an hour, or 0.1 hour, equals 6 minutes. So, 3×0.1, or 0.3 hours, would equal 18 minutes. When the students moved on to consider the time that a jet would take to travel the same 90 miles, they noted that the jet can travel 600 miles per hour. Several students reasoned that since the jet traveled twice as fast as the small airplane, its time must be half as long, or 0.15 hour, or 9 minutes.

Task 3—Is There a Giant in the House?

The final activity in the investigation focuses on giant-sized dimensions to explore multiplicative reasoning and develop the underpinnings of proportional reasoning, which will become increasingly important in the middle grades. As a springboard to this lesson, read aloud to the class a book such as *Jim and the Beanstalk* (Briggs 1970) or *Gulliver in Lilliput* (Hodges 1995).

Give each student a copy of the blackline master "Is There a Giant in the House?" In this task, the students consider their own size in relation to that of an imaginary giant who is 9 feet tall—slightly taller than Robert Wadlow (1918–1940), whose record still stands as the

In the children's book *Jim and the Beanstalk* (Briggs 1970), a climb up a beanstalk brings Jim to the home of an unhappy giant, who can't see to read his poetry, doesn't have teeth to eat, and has no hair and so feels ugly. Jim makes measurements that help the giant obtain eyeglasses, dentures, and a wig, immensely improving his life.

tallest man (8 feet, 11 inches) ever to live. Students can work on the task in groups or pairs (or alone with help from a classmate in determining such measurements as the length of one of their arms).

In step 1, the students measure their height, arm length, length of little finger, length of foot, and width of foot. Step 2 asks them to compare particular measurements multiplicatively. Although fifth graders have not studied proportions formally, they can make these comparisons with a bit of prompting. Help them build on their earlier work in the investigation by asking, for example, "How many feet would you need to line up end to end to equal your height?" (see fig. 21). Your students will probably be entertained or claim to be horrified at the idea of so many disembodied parts, but in either case you will have their attention.

Gulliver himself is a giant in the land of the six-inch Lilliputians in the children's book *Gulliver in Lilliput* (Hodges 1995), based on Jonathan Swift's classic, *Gulliver's Travels*.

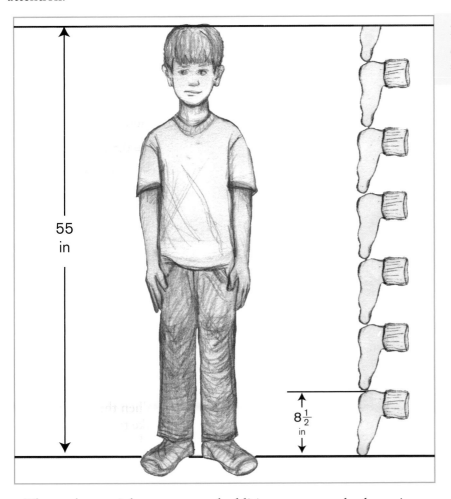

Fig. **21.**

Comparing a fifth grader's height and foot length

55 in

$8\frac{1}{2}$ in

The students might use repeated addition or repeated subtraction to answer your "how many" question. If, for example, a student's height is 55 inches, and his foot length is $8\frac{1}{2}$ inches, as in figure 21, the student might add $8\frac{1}{2}$ to itself again and again until the sum is just under or over 55 inches. Or he might begin with 55 inches and subtract $8\frac{1}{2}$ again and again until he has "used up" the 55 inches.

If you observe your students proceeding in either of these ways, help them associate what they are doing with multiplication or division.

For other books about giants to use in connection with measurement and scale, see "Using Literature as a Vehicle to Explore Proportional Reasoning" (Thompson, Austin, and Beckmann 2002; available on the CD-ROM).

Remind them that in using repeated addition or repeated subtraction, they are actually thinking multiplicatively.

Turn the students' attention to question 2(*a*) on the activity sheet: "Compare your height with the length of your arm by saying how many arm lengths would equal your height." Be sure to read aloud the hint that follows: "Your height is how many times the length of your arm?" Emphasize that the question "How many *times*?" calls for a comparison based on multiplication—not addition. A question calling for a comparison based on addition might be, "How many inches would you need to add to your arm length to equal your height?" or, alternatively, "What is the difference between your height and your arm length?"

As the students continue to think about one measurement being a certain number of times another measurement, some may come up with the idea of dividing to make the comparison between the two measurements. For example, they might take their height—say 55 inches—and divide it by the length of their foot—say, $8\frac{1}{2}$ inches—to find how many times their foot length goes into their height: $55 \div 8.5 \approx 6.5$.

If you think your students are ready for the concept of a *ratio*, explain that dividing 55 by 8.5 gives the ratio of 55 to 8.5—that is, the number of times that 55 contains 8.5. Students may see 6.5 more clearly as a ratio if you write the division as $\frac{55}{8.5} \approx \frac{6.5}{1}$ and read it as "55 is to 8.5 (approximately) as 6.5 is to 1."

Using this ratio, the student could compare the two measurements by saying that his height is approximately 6.5 times the length of his foot. Alternatively, the student could divide his foot length by his height ($8 \div 55$) to obtain the ratio 0.1454545.... Using this ratio, the student could compare the measurements by saying that his foot length is 0.1454545... times his height.

Discuss the multiplicative approaches of individual students with the whole class so that all the students have an opportunity to benefit from their classmates' discoveries. Thinking multiplicatively will prepare the students for the last section of task 3, in which they use their own measurements to calculate corresponding measurements of a giant who is 9 feet tall and proportioned exactly like themselves.

Students who understand how to determine a ratio between the giant's height (9 feet, or 108 inches) and their own—will be set to estimate the size of the giant's other attributes in step 3. A student whose height is 55 inches, for example, can divide 108 by 55, obtaining a ratio of approximately 1.96.

This student may need your help to see that 1.96 is the *multiplier*, or *scale factor*, that he can use to "up-size" his own measurements to obtain measurements for the giant. Explain that 1.96 tells *how many times* larger each gigantic attribute is than the corresponding attribute in the student. Thus, if the student's foot measures 8.5 inches in length, the giant's foot measures approximately 8.5 × 1.96, or 16.66, inches.

For step 4, give each student three sheets of inch grid paper. On one the students will trace an outline of their own foot, and then they will count squares in the grid to estimate the area of their footprint. They will use the other two sheets to make a full-size sketch of the giant's footprint. To have an unbroken grid large enough for the sketch, let

Be sure that your students understand that the scale factor applies to *all* measured dimensions. For example, if the *length* of the giant's foot is 1.96 times the length of the student's foot, then the *width* of the giant's foot is 1.96 times the width of the student's foot. As a result, the area of the giant's foot is 1.96^2, or about 3.84, times the area of the student's foot.

Navigating through Problem Solving and Reasoning in Grade 5

them trim borders and tape the two sheets together. Guide them as necessary as they develop sketches from the measurements that they computed in step 3 for the length and width of the giant's foot. They must count squares again to estimate the area of the giant's footprint.

Next, the students compare the giant's footprint with their own by saying how many times larger its area appears to be than that of their own foot footprint. Area is a square measure, and the students may see that the ratio of the areas approximates the square of the ratio of linear measurements (student's foot width to giant's foot width or student's foot length to giant's foot length).

In step 5, the students choose an everyday item, such as a comb, toothbrush, or pencil. Allow the students some flexibility in choosing an item. You might have them bring a common item from home.

If a student's object is long but not very wide, such as a cotton swab, then a linear model may be sufficient for a good sense of the giant-sized counterpart. The student could make a giant-sized model of a cotton swab with multilink cubes if you have a set in the classroom.

However, if the object is both long and wide, such as a comb or a toothbrush, have the students determine giant-sized dimensions for both length and width. Working with the area of such an object will again give the students an opportunity to see the squaring of the ratio of paired linear measurements that occurs in a ratio of area measurements. The area of the giant-sized object will be k^2 times the area of the student-sized object, where k is the multiplier between paired linear measurements such as the student's height and the giant's height.

In comparing the size of an implement that they use every day with the size of a suitable counterpart for the imaginary giant, the students are solving a problem that involves multiple steps:

1. They find the ratio of their height to the giant's height. (The attribute selected for comparison in the giant and the student need not be height, of course.)

2. They measure the length (and possibly other dimensions) of their implement.

3. They find the corresponding measurement(s) in a giant-sized version of the implement by using the ratio from step 1 as a multiplier for the measurement(s) from step 2.

This multistep process may not seem obvious or natural to many students, but with your guidance and careful questioning, they can use it successfully.

Assessment

Assessment should be an ongoing process as you observe your students making measurements and comparing them in the investigation. For more formal assessment, you could modify several of the questions on the activity sheets. For example, the activity sheet "Measuring Up with Animals" asks students to compare themselves with another animal or object in some way. You could pose other questions like these to make a formal assessment of the work of individual students or pairs of students.

Students need to learn to solve problems that involve multiple steps. Later, in middle school, they will "extend their work with ratios to develop an understanding of proportionality that they apply to solve single and multistep problems in numerous contexts." (NCTM 2006, p. 19).

You could also ask students to research an animal or object and reason multiplicatively to make a comparison between themselves and their animal or object on the basis of measurements. You might require the students to illustrate their comparison in some way, as the students did who compared their heights with the reach of a sun jelly-fish and the height of a giant sequoia tree.

The questions on the activity sheet "Is There a Giant in the House?" can also be the basis for a formal assessment. Students—individually, in pairs, or in small groups—can find measurements of everyday objects and determine appropriate measurements for giant-sized versions of the objects. If the students work in groups, encourage them to use chart paper to record their measures and show how they obtained the giant's measurements. In addition, students could build a model of the giant's object with manipulatives available in the classroom.

Reflections

Fifth graders have found these tasks engaging, particularly when the teacher has introduced the activity with a story. The tasks involve a range of measurement activities and concepts, including finding lengths and areas, estimating a distance and then comparing the estimate with an actual measure, recording time, and determining speed. Throughout the activities, students have many opportunities to be actively engaged in determining measures and using appropriate measurement tools.

At several points in these activities, students must solve problems that involve multiple steps. Students should work together on these problems so that they can discuss strategies and consider how to approach each problem.

Connections

This investigation connects mathematics directly with literature and language arts, science, and social studies. After completing task 1 (Measuring Up with Animals), students can investigate other attributes and characteristics of the animals, determining, for example, their geographic locations in the world, the areas of their habitats, and their typical food supplies. Task 2 (Getting from Here to There) also relates mathematics to social studies. You and your students can discuss such topics as the distances that children often walked to school during the years when the country was being settled. Students living on the plains might easily have walked several miles each way to school. You might also have your students consider how long it took people to travel west across the United States by covered wagon. *Wagon Wheels* (Brenner 1978) tells the story of a family that traveled from Kentucky to Kansas in the late 1800s in search of free land. The children in the story walked most of the way!

In addition, this investigation connects measurement with several of the other content strands in *Principles and Standards for School Mathematics* (NCTM 2000). In particular, students work with number and operations as they consider aspects of proportional reasoning. Students also work with geometry when they consider what it means for a giant-sized object to be similar to that of an ordinary person.

Which Month to Ski?

Focus

Reasoning about data relationships

Overview

This investigation engages students in summarizing data, making a decision based on data, and describing a procedure using data to make decisions in similar situations in the future. Working in groups of three, students examine the average daily snowfall at White Hills Ski Resort for the months of January, February, March, and April for two consecutive years. They rank these four months according to skiing conditions (from best to worst) to decide which month is best for a ski trip. The goal is to establish a procedure that the students could use to rerank the months in the future if they had additional, more recent data about daily snowfall to analyze.

Activities in the investigation help students—

- understand the real-world context of the problem;
- review requisite skills; and
- assess procedures for analyzing data to solve the problem.

To become acquainted with the context, the students read a piece in the format of a newspaper article about skiing for the first time. Working alone, they answer "readiness" questions that help them think about the context and review what they know about interpreting data in a table.

Students complete the snowfall investigation in small groups. When the class reconvenes, each group presents its ranking of the four months and explains its procedure for ranking the months. The other students ask questions and provide feedback on the group's ranking procedure. Each group has the opportunity to make revisions to its procedure before the students submit their work for formal assessment by the teacher.

Goals

- Analyze and compare data to solve a problem by making a decision
- Examine a process for analyzing data to develop a decision-making procedure for future use
- Reevaluate and revise a procedure in response to self-assessment, peer assessment, and other feedback

Mathematical Content

This investigation supports the following Data Analysis and Probability and Process Standards and expectations for grades 3–5 (NCTM 2000, pp. 176, 402).

The development of this activity was supported by the School Mathematics and Science Center (SMSC), Purdue University, West Lafayette, Indiana, under the direction of Richard Lesh.

"As students learn to describe the similarities and differences between data sets, they will have an opportunity to develop clear descriptions of the data and to formulate conclusions and arguments based on the data." (NCTM 2000, p. 177)

Providing a challenging investigation to small groups of students facilitates ongoing reasoning, argument, and assessment throughout the problem-solving process.

Data Analysis and Probability

- Select and use appropriate statistical methods to analyze data
  - Describe the shape and important features of a set of data and compare related data sets, with an emphasis on how the data are distributed
  - Use measures of center … and understand what each does and does not indicate about the data set
  - Compare different representations of the same data and evaluate how well each representation shows important aspects of the data
- Develop and evaluate inferences and predictions that are based on data
  - Propose and justify conclusions and predictions that are based on data
- Understand and apply basic concepts of probability
  - Describe events as likely or unlikely and discuss the degree of likelihood

Problem Solving

- Build new mathematical knowledge through problem solving
- Solve problems that arise in mathematics and in other contexts
- Apply and adapt a variety of appropriate strategies to solve problems

Reasoning and Proof

- Make and investigate mathematical conjectures
- Develop and evaluate mathematical arguments and proofs
- Select and use various types of reasoning and methods of proof

Communication

- Communicate … mathematical thinking coherently and clearly to peers, teachers, and others

The initial ideas about analyzing data that students develop in this investigation are essential for making decisions based on sets of real-world data gathered in everyday situations. The students analyze data on daily snowfall for four months over a two-year period to determine which month is likely to offer the best skiing conditions. They may select different data and work with them in different ways, depending on the approach that they take. They might use all the data to rank the months on the basis of average snowfall per day, or they might simply find the average number of days that snow falls in a given month. Alternatively, they might decide to filter out, or ignore, data from days when no snow falls and find the average snowfall on the days when snow does fall.

Statisticians sometimes make use of *stochastic processes*—families of random variables that can be indexed against some other variable or set of variables and analyzed, though not precisely predicted. Statisticians may rank data according to one set of variables and then rerank them according to a secondary set of variables. In this investigation, students may use a simplified version of this approach when they first rank the months by using one procedure and then—for example, to settle "ties" between two months having about the same average daily snowfall—establish a second procedure for modifying the first ranking.

Students go beyond ranking the four months to develop and describe a generalizable data-analysis procedure that the Brown County Youth Club could apply to future data. Requiring students to communicate an approach that someone else might use with other, similar data sets is comparable to solving real-world problems by using mathematical models to predict outcomes, explain data, or rank likelihoods.

Prior Knowledge or Experience

- Work with whole-unit linear measures (e.g., inches, centimeters)
- Experience in interpreting data in simple tables
- Experience in comparing and ordering numbers of up to three digits
- Work with whole and decimal numbers (including computations with a calculator or by hand)

Materials

For each student—

- A copy of each of the following blackline masters:
  - "Skiing for the First Time?"
  - "What Do You Know about It Now?"
  - "Which Month to Ski?"
  - "Another Year of Snow"
- Paper and pencil
- A four-function calculator
- A sheet of centimeter grid paper (template available on p. 90)
- Computers with word processing and spreadsheet software (optional)

For the teacher—

- Overhead transparencies and transparency markers or pens (optional)

Classroom Environment

The students work in groups of three at clustered desks or tables. The initial work by the small groups will take approximately one hour. Group presentations to the class and subsequent revisions to procedures are important parts of the investigation.

Investigation

To begin the investigation, give each student a copy of the blackline master "Skiing for the First Time?" and the blackline master "What Do You Know about It Now?" The first activity sheet presents information about skiing in the format of a newspaper article, covering what beginning skiers need to consider before they go on a skiing trip. After the

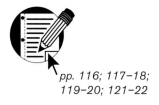

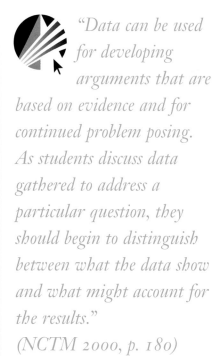

students have finished reading the article, have them work by themselves to complete the readiness questions on the second activity sheet, "What Do You Know about It Now?" Responding to these questions will help the students review that they have learned from the article and refurbish some important prerequisite skills—for example, how to read information from a table. Use the students' responses as the basis for a class discussion about skiing, the information in the table, and why skiers' slogan is "Think snow!"

Give each student a copy of the blackline master "Which Month to Ski?" This activity sheet presents the scenario and related problem that the students must investigate. Read the scenario aloud to the class, and direct the students' attention to the accompanying table (see fig. 22).

Next, read aloud the problem statement, which follows:

> The Brown County Youth Club needs your help in deciding which month to choose for its skiing trip. Scheduling difficulties may rule out Saturdays in the group's first-choice month, so the club is asking you to rank the four months from "best" to "worst" – that is, from most likely to least likely to offer good snow for skiing. Write a letter to the Brown County Youth Club with your rankings, and explain how you made your decisions.
>
> Also, the youth group might decide to make this ski trip an annual event. If so, the members might want to use your method to reconsider their choice of the best month to ski in future years, when they would have additional daily snowfall data to analyze. As a result, the club would like a step-by-step description of your method for making a decision and ranking the months.

Remind the students that they must analyze data for several purposes:
- To compare snowfalls for four months (January, February, March, and April) over a two-year period

Fig. **22.**

The skiing scenario and table of data

Which Month to Ski?

Name _____

Last summer, as a community service project, the Brown County Youth Club helped clean the roadsides along Highway 68, which leads to White Hills Ski Resort. To thank the youth group for its work, the resort has invited members of the group to come and ski, free of charge, on a Saturday of their choosing in the next January, February, March, or April. The group wants to narrow down its decision to the month that is likely to have the most snow. Thus, the group has asked White Hills Ski Resort for information about its daily snowfall during these months in past years. The club received the following table of information from the resort for the ski months in the years 2004 and 2005.

Daily Snowfall (in Inches) at White Hills Ski Resort
January–April, 2004–2005

Day	JANUARY 2004	JANUARY 2005	FEBRUARY 2004	FEBRUARY 2005	MARCH 2004	MARCH 2005	APRIL 2004	APRIL 2005
1	2	0	3	0	0	3	1	0
2	0	0	1	1	7	2	2	2
3	0	1	4	3	8	1	1	0
4	0	3	5	4	3	3	2	0
5	4	4	0	7	4	9	2	0
6	0	5	0	1	0	0	0	4
7	1	0	4	0	0	0	1	5
8	1	1	3	0	1	5	3	4
9	0	0	4	0	5	6	1	3
10	0	2	5	0	4	1	2	2
11	5	3	0	8	2	2	3	2
12	1	0	0	4	3	1	2	0
13	4	0	10	5	8	4	0	3
14	0	0	1	0	0	0	0	2
15	0	1	2	1	3	2	2	3
16	0	0	0	5	2	0	0	4
17	1	0	2	2	1	2	2	0
18	0	0	4	3	1	0	0	4
19	3	4	6	0	0	1	2	0
20	0	2	0	1	0	0	3	2
21	2	0	0	6	0	0	1	2
22	3	4	1	4	0	1	0	1
23	0	3	2	4	2	5	0	2
24	0	0	1	1	5	0	1	0
25	1	1	6	0	3	1	2	6
26	1	0	4	0	4	4	5	0
27	0	0	4	3	8	0	2	1
28	3	0	0	0	2	0	0	2
29	5	1	0	------	0	0	1	1
30	0	1	------	------	4	3	0	0
31	0	2	------	------	1	1	-----	-----

- To rank the four months, January through April, from best to worst for skiing
- To develop a procedure, based on the data, for analyzing additional data in the future and reranking the same months for skiing on the basis of the new data

Say to the students, "The Brown County Youth Club is asking you for a product. Can you describe the product that you must create?" Give the students a hint by telling them that this product has two parts. (It has a ranking of the four months with the given data and a method for ranking the months that can be used on other data sets.) Then emphasize the function of the product by asking the students, "Who will be using this product?" (The Brown County Youth Club)

Assign the students to groups of three, and explain that they will work in these groups to analyze the data and rank the months. Then each group will make a presentation to the class in which the group members will—

- share their rankings of the months;
- describe their procedure in a general way so that someone can use it with new data in future years; and

• explain why their procedure will result in a ranking that reliably identifies the month that is likely to offer the best skiing.

Encourage the students to ask questions about the steps in each group's procedure. Is each step clear? Taken together, are the steps adequate? When students handle problems of this type by working together in groups, they tend to go through productive cycles of revising, retesting, and refining procedures very naturally.

For example, one group of students approached the problem by finding the total snowfall for each of the four months. However, as one of the students pointed out, "This won't work, because March has more days than February!" This revelation eventually led the group to find the average snowfall per day in each of the months.

In another group that began by finding the total snowfall for each month, one student commented, "I think that it is more important to have fresh snow almost every day than it is just to have a lot of snow on some days." Prompted by this suggestion, the group developed a new way of defining "best month to ski." They decided that skiing conditions in a month depended on the average snowfall on "snow days" during the month—that is, the days when snow actually fell. Although this interpretation reintroduced the problem of the months' different numbers of days, the group worked out this problem by using ratios or percentages.

The cycle of discussing, testing, and revising led the students in the first group to consider a more sophisticated and appropriate procedure—one that takes more variables into account. This process also led the students in the second group to narrow and refine their definition of "best month to ski," which in turn altered their approach to the problem.

Sample solutions follow from two groups of fifth graders who worked on the problem. Note that your students use the same daily snowfall data, January–April, that these students used. However, the investigation in this book renumbers the years for which the data are given, in the interest of updating the material for the students. The former fifth graders produced the samples discussed here on the basis of daily snowfall data said to be from the years 1998 and 1999 (extended data sets included 2000 and 2001). The investigation presented for your students updates each of these years by six years (for example, data originally said to be for 1998 are now presented as data for 2004, adjusting for the fact that 2004 was a leap year and 1998 was not). However, all samples of past work by students use the earlier set of years.

Sample Solution 1

One group of students initially defined "best month to ski" as the month with the greatest average snowfall per day. Later, this group formulated a second definition. The students decided that the best month for skiing was the month with the greatest average snowfall per day on the days when snow fell. The group members were unable to reach consensus on which definition to use, so they decided to work with both. They constructed a double-bar graph that was similar to that in figure 23.

To determine the height of the bars representing the average snowfall per day in a month—that is, the average for all the days of the

When students work on challenging problems in small groups, their dialogue reveals their thinking and gives teachers excellent opportunities to assess their reasoning.

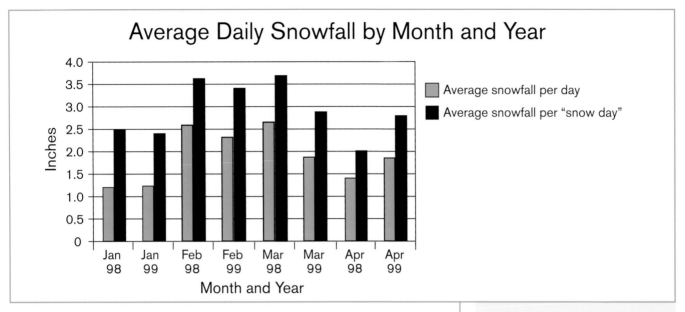

Average Daily Snowfall by Month and Year

Inches

Month and Year

Average snowfall per day

Average snowfall per "snow day"

month—the students divided the total snowfall for the month by the number of days in that month. For example, for January of the first year, they divided 37 (the number of inches of snowfall that month) by 31 (the number of days in the month). To determine the height of the bars representing average snowfall per snow day—that is, the average daily snowfall only for days when snow actually fell, they divided the total snowfall by the total snow days. For example, for the first year's January, they divided 37 (the total inches of snowfall for the month) by 15 (the number of days on which snow fell).

The group found it difficult to use the graph in figure 23 to determine whether February or March, over the two-year period, had the greater average daily snowfall (either overall or just for snow days), and thus, they found it difficult to establish which was the better month to ski. This difficulty led them to combine the data for the two years in a new graph, as shown in figure 24.

To determine the height of each bar representing the average daily snowfall for a month, the group totaled the daily snowfall in a particular month for the two years in which data were collected. Then they

Fig. **23.**

A double-bar graph showing average snowfall per day and average snowfall per "snow day" (a day when snow fell) for January–April over a two-year period

Fig. **24.**

A double-bar graph showing average snowfall per day and average snowfall per "snow day" (a day when snow actually falls) for January–April (on the basis of data for two years)

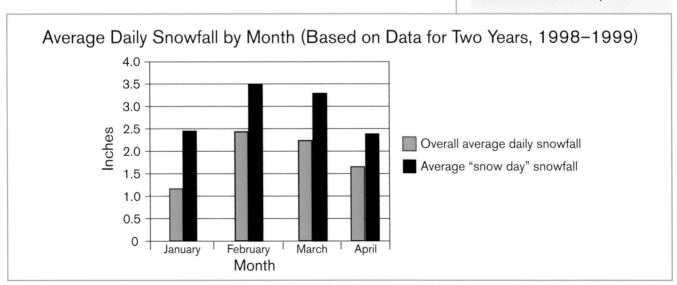

Average Daily Snowfall by Month (Based on Data for Two Years, 1998–1999)

Inches

Month

Overall average daily snowfall

Average "snow day" snowfall

doubled the number of days in the month (to work with all the days in that month in the two years, with neither year adding a day in February for a leap year). Finally, they divided the total daily snowfall by this doubled number. Thus, for January the students combined the 1998 and 1999 daily snowfalls to get 75 inches, and then they divided this total by two times the number of days in January (2×31, 62; $75 \div 62 = 1.2$ inches).

To determine the height of each bar representing the overall average daily snowfall for snow days for a month, the students divided the total snowfall for that month, over the two years in which data were collected, by the total number of days when snow fell in the month, over those two years. For example, for January, the students divided the total daily snowfall (75 inches) by the total number of snow days in the two years ($15 + 16 = 31$ snow days; $75 \div 31 = 2.4$ inches).

A graph similar to that in figure 24 prompted the students to rank the months as follows on the basis of the overall average snowfall per day in a month (from the highest average to the lowest):

1. February
2. March
3. April
4. January

The students ranked the months in a different way on the basis of the average snowfall per snow day in a month (highest to lowest):

1. February
2. March
3. January
4. April

The students were struck by the fact that the rankings were not the same for the two methods. Because January and April seemed to be in a "close tie" for average daily snowfall for snow days, the group decided to use the overall average daily snowfall for its final ranking of the months.

The students were successful in generalizing the procedure that they followed to determine this ranking. The letter that they wrote to the Brown County Youth Club describing their method appears in figure 25. (Note that the letter does not provide the group's ranking of the months.)

This sample solution, a high-level response for fifth graders, reveals a number of strengths. First, it clearly links an appropriate mathematical and statistical procedure to two different definitions of "best month to ski":

• The month, January–April, that has the greatest average snowfall per day
• The month, January–April, that has the greatest average snowfall per snow day (a day when snow actually falls)

Second, by using the *average* daily snowfall, the solution accommodates the varying number of days in each month. It also successfully combines data over a number of years. Finally, the students' mathematical communication about their process for finding these two types of

Dear Brown County Youth Club,

To find the month with greatest amount of snow, which will be best month for skiing, take these steps:

1. Find the total snowfall for all Januarys, all Februarys, all Marches, and all Aprils.

2. Find the total number of days for all Januarys, all Februarys, all Marches, and all Aprils.

3. Divide the total snowfall for each month by the total number of days in that month to determine the heights of the bars that show the overall average daily snowfall.

4. Find the total number of days in all Januarys, all Februarys, all Marches, and all Aprils that had snowfall.

5. Divide the total snowfall for each month by the total number of days that had snowfall for that month to determine the height of the bars that show average snowfall on snow days.

Sincerely,
The Data Consultants

averages is excellent—they provide a clear step-by-step procedure that is general enough to ensure that others can use it in approaching different sets of data.

The group members could make a number of improvements to their final product—the letter to the Brown County Youth Club. First and foremost, they should have included their rankings of the months. In addition, they would have strengthened their letter if they had incorporated some of the procedures that they actually used during their own problem-solving process. For example, they might have described how to create graphs as a visual representation of the averages. Such graphs make it easy to rank the months.

Furthermore, the students might have included in their general procedure a suggestion about how to break ties, even though they developed a situation-specific method for tie breaking. Anticipating the client's needs and providing complete descriptions of the mathematical procedures present a challenge to students, but they can succeed (see sample solution 2 below).

You can help your students become more skillful in communicating mathematically by posing questions to them as if you were the client. For example, a teacher could respond to this group's work by writing the letter that appears in figure 26.

Fig. 26.

A letter suggesting improvements to the students' product in figure 25, from a teacher posing as a representative of the Brown County Youth Club

Dear Data Consultants,

It is clear from your directions how we can use two different averages to determine the best month for skiing in the future. But we don't know what to do with the averages once we have computed them. Please tell us how we can use the averages to rank the months. How did you rank the months for the data you had? Also, what should we do if there is a tie between the averages for two of the months?

Sincerely,
The Brown County Youth Club

Sample Solution 2

Another group of students attempted to combine the same two definitions of "best month to ski"—the month that has the greatest average snowfall per day, and the month that has the greatest average snowfall per snow day (day when snow actually falls). The letter that these students wrote to the Brown County Youth Club appears in figure 27.

This sample solution has all the strengths of the first solution and additional advantages, as well. The students successfully articulated their process of summing the rankings that they assigned to the averages for daily snowfall, as determined for the two definitions of "best month to ski." They also provided clear direction on what to do with the totals to make a final ranking. Their letter also describes what to do in case of a tie.

Fig. 27.

A letter from students acting as data consultants to the Brown County Youth Club

Dear Brown County Youth Club,

To rank the months for skiing, we first found the overall average snowfall for all days in the month for both years combined. Then we averaged the snowfall only for snow days for both years combined. We made this table with the data (we rounded to the closest hundredth of an inch):

	January	February	March	April
Overall average daily snowfall (in inches)	1.21	2.41	2.23	1.60
Average snow-day snowfall (in inches)	2.42	3.55	3.30	2.34

Then we assigned a rank to each month for each average in the table (1 for best month to ski and 4 for worst month to ski). Then we added up the rankings, so that the month with the smallest sum would be the best choice. Here is a table that shows how we did this:

	January	February	March	April
Ranking for overall average daily snowfall	4	1	2	3
Ranking for average snow-day snowfall	3	1	2	4
Rankings added together	7	2	4	7

January and April tied for last, so we decided to choose the month with the higher average snow-day snowfall. So our order was February, March, January, and then April. You can use the same method on your new sets of data.

Sincerely,
Gene, LaTanya, and Chris

To help these student consultants improve on this already very high-level response, the teacher could write a letter like that in figure 28.

Dear Gene, LaTanya, and Chris,

You have given us a very clear description of how we should analyze the data when we get more recent snowfall information. Thank you. We have one question: Because you used average snowfall per snow day to break the tie, does that mean that your preferred best definition for "best month to ski" is the month that has the greatest average snowfall per snow day? And if so, why not simply use the snow-day procedure to rank the months in the first place?

Sincerely,
The Brown County Youth Club

Fig. **28.**

A teacher posing as a member of the Brown County Youth Club to offer feedback to students on the solution in figure 27

Assessment

Group members' presentations of their letters to the Brown County Youth Club provide opportunities for both peer assessment and self-assessment. When a group presents its procedure for analyzing data and determining a ranking of the months, you might ask the other students to apply the procedure by analyzing the extended data set in the black-line master "Another Year of Snow." The table on this activity sheet presents the 2004 and 2005 January–April daily snowfall data that the students have already examined, along with daily snowfall data for January–April in 2006.

The students will begin to pose questions to the presenters and make suggestions very naturally as they work with the new data. Their feedback will help the presenters clarify and amplify their approach, increasing its effectiveness. The other students may offer specific ideas to help the presenting group revise its letter. As suggested earlier, you can evaluate the groups' final products—their letters to the Brown County Youth Club—by taking the role of a spokesperson for the club and asking questions or commenting on the work.

Your students can also use this technique to critique the work by students that appears on the accompanying CD-ROM. Make transparencies of these samples of students' work, and share them with your students. Together, you and your students can act as members of the

Samples of fifth graders' work on "Which Month to Ski?" appear on the CD-ROM. You can make transparencies of this work to share with your students.

Brown County Youth Club and assess the work. The students can compose response letters to the student data consultants in the sample work, indicating areas that they need to clarify or improve. You and your students can then decide together what criteria to use to grade the final products. Be sure to point out that although these fifth graders worked with the same data that your students used, their data were said to be for a set of earlier years—1998 and 1999 instead of 2004 and 2005.

An investigation like Which Month to Ski? may be a new experience for many students, and they may need to complete a few such investigations and share in several subsequent assessments to learn what constitutes good work. For this reason, some teachers evaluate students' group work in early investigations on the basis of its completeness or the students' participation. You and your students can use grading guidelines that you develop together—the students can use them for self-grading and peer grading, and you can use them for grading your students' work.

Reflections

This investigation incorporates thinking and reasoning processes for using data to make real-world decisions. Successful solutions involve refining and clarifying problems, approaches, and results. For example, deciding which month is best for skiing depends on coming up with a precise definition of "best month to ski." Does this term designate the month in which the average daily snowfall is the greatest? Does it signify the month in which the average snowfall per "snow day" is the greatest? Or does it denote something else entirely?

Moreover, solutions to such problems are almost always associated with cycles of expressing, testing, and revising procedures and results. For example, students may at first simply total the daily snowfall for each month. However, through cycles of revision, their accounting methods become increasingly precise, and they coordinate more of the relevant variables in the problem—for instance, the different numbers of days in the months. To deal with this variation, one group found the average snowfall per day, while another group excluded from the total snowfall for a month the snow that fell on the 29th, 30th, and 31st days of any month.

Although interactions among students and cycles of revision usually lead to improved final products, two types of misconceptions surfaced in classes that completed this investigation. One type is related to the students' general lack of familiarity with complex problems, and the other type is related to their uncertainty about how to handle a complex problem in the specific context at hand. Students must recognize that in general complex problems have more than one correct response, and they must also recognize that such problems call for formulations in particular real-world contexts. As a result, problem solvers must determine and refine *on their own* the mathematical questions that they must answer. Before grasping these ideas, students may have a variety of misconceptions, several examples of which follow:

- Students may expect an investigation to conclude with only one correct method for making a decision. If so, they may become frustrated. They may resist engaging in the problem or feel at a loss because the problem formulation required in the investigation seems overwhelming. To help students overcome this misconception, emphasize that there are a number of good ways to work through the investigation and that real-world scientific experiments often use a number of good methods for making final recommendations. In this investigation, the students could use multiple representations—tables and graphs—to display the data to support their final decision. Working in small groups also helps students persevere and stay engaged.

- Students may expect to identify and use a mathematical or statistical procedure that they have learned previously. Students who have limited experience with problems that require them to go through multiple cycles of expressing, testing, and revising their ideas may be frustrated when they find that they need to modify their initial method of analyzing the data repeatedly during the collaborative problem-solving process. Although initial solutions to problems are posed, tested, and modified frequently in everyday life, students are often surprised to find this process occurring in mathematics class. Assure your students that revising and modifying their initial ideas are activities that you expect and that are important for their learning. As students engage in more investigations like these, they will begin to recognize that cycles of development and revision are a natural and constructive part of the problem-solving process.

- One group of students may find the mean of all the data for a particular month (for example, the mean of snowfall in January for the years for which they have data), and another group may find the average daily snowfall for each month. Although the first method is reasonable, the second method is more sophisticated and useful in the context, because it takes into account the varying

The activity sheet "Four Years of Snow," available on the CD-ROM, provides a table of daily snowfall data for January–April over a four-year period (2004–2007). This extended data set is also available on the CD-ROM in an Excel spreadsheet, which students can manipulate electronically if they have classroom access to the software.

numbers of days in the months January–April. Thus, the second method allows for direct comparisons among months. Furthermore, finding the mean of all the data in a particular month is less effective since in the scenario data are available for only two years. If data were available for more years (as in the extended data set, "Four Years of Snow," on the CD-ROM), this approach would be more effective. In one classroom, finding the mean of all the data in a month turned out to be a good preliminary solution, because as the students articulated and tested it, they often revised it. Sometimes revisions did not occur until after the group had made its presentation. Students gained insights from the other groups' procedures and used those ideas to revise their own approach, highlighting the potential for students to learn from one another.

Connections

This investigation supports connections within mathematics and across the curriculum. Connecting mathematical ideas, students use number sense and arithmetic skills as they solve the problem. They also learn the basics of exploratory data analysis as they devise and revise procedures, apply them, critique them, and revise them again. They are likely to use various representations of the data in the procedures they develop. Further, the notion of *generalization*, not commonly incorporated in fifth-grade curricula, comes into play when the students develop a procedure that can be applied to new data sets.

The students forge connections across the curriculum as they read the newspaper article and respond to the readiness questions. These activities could easily take place in the context of reading and language arts instruction. The students' presentations of their ranking procedures place a heavy emphasis on mathematical communication (oral, visual, and written), a skill that can be addressed in both language arts and mathematics classes.

Subsequent follow-up activities can help students develop their data-analysis procedures and decision-making capabilities:

- Have each group apply its own procedure and one other group's procedure to the information in the blackline master "Another Year of Snow." The application of different procedures allows the students to practice various skills while also testing and making suggestions for improving the procedures.

- Have students learn to use spreadsheet software by applying their procedures to the Excel database, "Four Years of Snow," on the CD-ROM. In addition, students can readily produce graphs to show the results of their procedures. Thus, they learn how to use different representations appropriately to communicate different aspects of the data sets.

- Have the students adapt their procedure for determining the best month to ski to other situations influenced by weather conditions, such as the best month to visit a particular beach. (The students could obtain data on rainfall or cloudiness by searching the Internet, thus learning to work simultaneously with categorical and numerical data.)

Making decisions based on an analysis of data and generalizing data-based procedures for future decision making are important aspects of statistics education and mathematical modeling. This investigation prepares students to approach other mathematical problems in the real world. Even fifth graders can begin to engage in data analysis and mathematical modeling, thus forming intuitions that will help them understand the concepts of statistics and probability that they encounter in secondary school and college. Further, such investigations give students a chance to apply their knowledge of numbers and engage in problem solving and reasoning in new and interesting ways, stretching their thinking to develop mathematical approaches that they can remember and reuse in the future.

PROBLEM SOLVING *and* REASONING

Looking Back and Looking Ahead

The investigations in this book emphasize problem solving and reasoning in the content strands of the mathematics curriculum—number and operations, algebra, geometry, measurement, and data analysis and probability. The explorations have been designed to stimulate students to think and reason while solving interesting problems.

Problem solving is the cornerstone of all school mathematics, prekindergarten–grade 12. Concepts and computational skills are not very useful if they are not accompanied by the ability to solve problems. A student who can divide accurately but cannot recognize a situation that calls for division is very limited as a problem solver.

The goal of all school mathematics is to enable all students to use facts, concepts, and procedures to solve increasingly challenging problems as they progress in school. Students in grades 3–6 should have daily experiences with problems that interest them and challenge them to think about various ideas in mathematical contexts. Good problems and problem-solving situations encourage both reasoning and communication. They stimulate students to exchange ideas with one another and with their teachers. These experiences also challenge students to develop and apply strategies, introduce them to new concepts, and provide a context for applying the skills that they have learned.

Teachers can help students become good problem solvers by selecting appropriate problems, giving students time to think and develop solution strategies, encouraging them to discuss their ideas, and assessing their understanding of the mathematics involved. Because good problems are challenging, students may encounter difficulty in arriving at solutions. Teachers must decide when their own input is necessary and when it is not. It is important for teachers and students to realize that challenging problems take time and that perseverance is necessary.

Students in grades 3–6 are poised to make important transitions in their reasoning. Until this time, many students have believed that something is always true if they have seen one or more examples of it. Now students learn that several examples are not sufficient to establish the general truth of a conjecture, and they discover that a single counterexample can show that a conjecture is not true.

Upper elementary students also need to learn what constitutes an acceptable explanation. Teachers must encourage them to explain and justify their thinking and help them learn how to detect fallacies in other students' thinking. Students should also move from considering individual mathematical objects (*this* triangle) to thinking about classes of objects (*all* triangles).

The process of problem solving and reasoning is not learned at any particular grade level but unfolds, deepens, and grows each year. As students enter the middle grades, they should have a sound mathematical foundation on which they can build mathematics that is more challenging than anything that they have encountered before.

All mathematics educators aim to teach more mathematics and to teach it better. To do so, they must model good problem-solving strategies and exhibit logical reasoning in the classroom. Students whose teachers are exemplary role models will be positively disposed toward mathematics.

GRADE 5

PROBLEM SOLVING *and* REASONING

Appendix

Blackline Masters and Solutions

Can You Divide It Evenly?

Name _____

Complete the chart by entering "Y" for *yes* if you can divide the number on the left evenly by the divisor at the head of the column. Leave the cell blank if the divisor does not divide the number evenly.

Divided by / Number	2?	3?	4?	5?	6?	8?	9?	10?
1								
2								
3								
4								
5								
6								
7								
8								
9								
10								
11								
12								

Can You Divide It Evenly? (continued)

Name _____

Divided by Number	2?	3?	4?	5?	6?	8?	9?	10?
13								
14								
15								
16								
17								
18								
19								
20								
21								
22								
23								
24								
25								
26								
27								
28								

Can You Divide It Evenly? (continued)

Name _____

Divided by Number	2?	3?	4?	5?	6?	8?	9?	10?
29								
30								
31								
32								
33								
34								
35								
36								
37								
38								
39								
40								
41								
42								
43								
44								

Navigating through Problem Solving and Reasoning in Grade 5

Can You Divide It Evenly? (continued)

Name _____

Divided by Number	2?	3?	4?	5?	6?	8?	9?	10?
45								
46								
47								
48								
49								
50								
51								
52								
53								
54								
55								
56								
57								
58								
59								
60								

Can You Divide It Evenly? (continued)

Name _____

Divided by / Number	2?	3?	4?	5?	6?	8?	9?	10?
61								
62								
63								
64								
65								
66								
67								
68								
69								
70								
71								
72								
73								
74								
75								
76								

Navigating through Problem Solving and Reasoning in Grade 5

Can You Divide It Evenly? (continued)

Name _____

Divided by / Number	2?	3?	4?	5?	6?	8?	9?	10?
77								
78								
79								
80								
81								
82								
83								
84								
85								
86								
87								
88								
89								
90								
91								
92								

Can You Divide It Evenly? (continued)

Name _____

Number \ Divided by	2?	3?	4?	5?	6?	8?	9?	10?
93								
94								
95								
96								
97								
98								
99								
100								

Navigating through Problem Solving and Reasoning in Grade 5

How Do You Know It's Divisible?

Name _____

What is true about all the numbers that are evenly divisible by 2? By 3? And so on, all the way up to 10 (except for 7)? Use the chart below to help you discover answers to these questions. In column 2, you will enter examples of numbers that are divisible by each divisor in column 1. Then you will consider what your examples have in common and write your discoveries in column 3. When you have completed the chart, your data in each row will let you complete the sentence,

"If a number is divisible by □, such as the numbers _____, then the number has

the following characteristic(s): _____."

If a number is divisible by	Such as the numbers	Then the number has these characteristics
2		
3		
4		

continued on the next page

Name _____

If a number is divisible by	Such as the numbers	Then the number has these characteristics
5		
6		
8		
9		
10		

A PIN for Mr. Mitchell

Name _____

Mr. Mitchell has just installed a new security system at his house. He must create a secret six-digit personal identification number, or PIN, as his password for the system. He decides to use the six digits in his date of birth: 05-24-76. It is very important to Mr. Mitchell that no one else discover his PIN, so he decides to rearrange the digits in a six-digit number that no one is likely to guess. After much thought, Mr. Mitchell decides to rearrange the numerals so that, from the left—

- the first digit is the largest of all the digits;
- the number formed by the first two digits is divisible by 2;
- the number formed by the first three digits is divisible by 3;
- the number formed by the first four digits is divisible by 4;
- the number formed by the first five digits is divisible by 5; and
- the entire six-digit number is divisible by 6.

Mr. Mitchell needs your help in creating a six-digit number that meets all of these conditions. By using the six digits in Mr. Mitchell's date of birth, can you create a PIN for him?

Pin number for Mr. Mitchell

Carina's Pet Sales

Name _____

Carina opened a pet store in town three weeks ago. Since her shop opened, she has seen her sales of guinea pigs, gerbils, and hamsters increase each week. Pet-store owners in other towns have told Carina that she can expect sales of these pets to continue increasing for the next five weeks as her shop becomes established. Carina wants to figure out how many guinea pigs, gerbils, and hamsters she is likely to sell over the next five weeks so that she can stock appropriate numbers of pets of each type.

Carina checks her records and finds that she has entered the following notes:

2 guinea pigs sold during week 1

4 guinea pigs sold during week 2

6 guinea pigs sold during week 3

Three times as many gerbils as guinea pigs sold each week, week 1 to week 3.

From week 1 to week 3, half as many hamsters sold each week as gerbils.

Other owners say to expect this pattern in guinea pig sales to continue over the next 5 weeks.

Owners say patterns in sales of gerbils and hamsters are also likely to go on for 5 more weeks.

Can you help Carina figure out how many guinea pigs, gerbils, and hamsters she is likely to sell in each of the next five weeks?

Navigating through Problem Solving and Reasoning in Grade 5

Projecting from Patterns

Name _____

Suppose that Carina has hired you and your partner as her accountants. Can you help her figure out how many guinea pigs, gerbils, and hamsters she will need to have in stock each week to satisfy her customers over the next five weeks?

Begin by using Carina's notes from weeks 1–3 (see the activity page "Carina's Pet Sales") to complete the following tables:

Weekly Sales of Guinea Pigs, Gerbils, and Hamsters

Week	Guinea Pig Sales
1	
2	
3	
4	
5	
6	
7	
8	

Week	Gerbil Sales
1	
2	
3	
4	
5	
6	
7	
8	

Week	Hamster Sales
1	
2	
3	
4	
5	
6	
7	
8	

Carina also wants you to provide her with graphs that show actual and projected sales of guinea pigs, gerbils, and hamsters for the first eight weeks that her shop is in business. Your teacher has given you centimeter grid paper and pencils or markers in three colors. Use these materials to create coordinate graphs to represent the numbers of guinea pigs, gerbils, and hamsters that Carina's shop will sell each week, from week 1 through week 8. Use a different colored pencil or marker for each type of pet. Make colored dots on your graphs to show the data. Be sure to title each graph and label your axes, and be prepared to explain all your tables

Centimeter Grid Paper

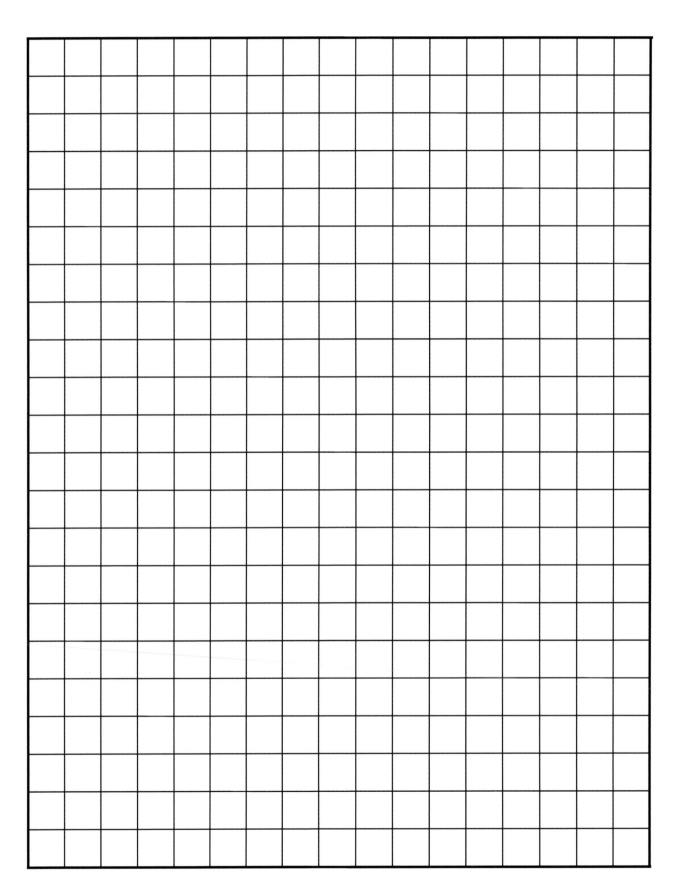

Navigating through Problem Solving and Reasoning in Grade 5

Animal Accounting

Name _____

1. Inspect your tables on the activity sheet "Projecting from Patterns." Suppose that *n* stands for the number of weeks that Carina's pet shop has been in business. (For example, if *n* = 1, the shop has been open for one week, if *n* = 2, it has been open for two weeks, and so on.) Use *n* to write a mathematical expression for each of the following:

   a. The number of guinea pig sales each week = _____

   b. The number of gerbil sales each week = _____

   c. The number of hamster sales each week = _____

2. Other pet-store owners have told Carina that her sales patterns in the first three weeks for guinea pigs, gerbils, and hamsters will continue over the next five weeks as her shop becomes established. After week 8, the rates are likely to change — probably leveling off. But suppose that Carina's rates in the first three weeks actually continue through week 20.

   a. How many guinea pigs would Carina expect to sell in week 18? _____

   b. How did you find your answer?

   c. How many gerbils would Carina expect to sell in week 20? _____

   d. How did you find your answer?

3. Below are three graphs that show sales patterns for three other pets in Carina's shop.

Graph 1

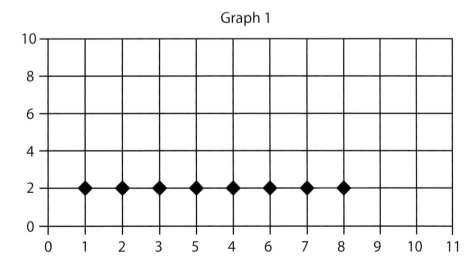

Name _____

Graph 2

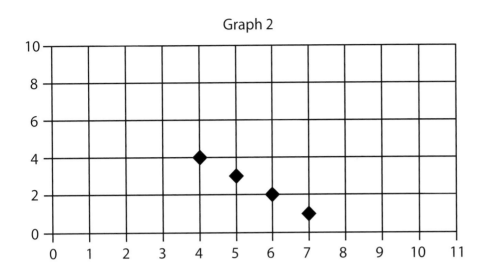

Graph 3

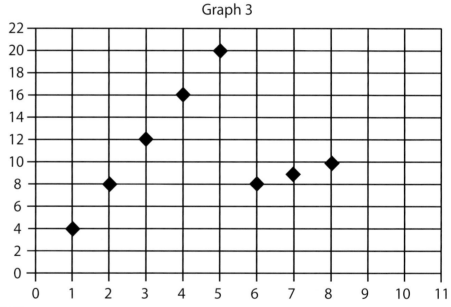

Read the descriptions on the next page of the three sales situations that the graphs show. Match each situation with the appropriate graph, and explain why the situation and the graph match.

Name _____

Sales situation 1

When Carina arrived at her shop at the beginning of week 4, she found a large box containing 10 kittens at her front door. Carina set up a sales area where she could display the kittens together and let them play. In the first week, Carina sold 4 kittens. In the second week, she sold 3 kittens, and in the third week, she sold 2 kittens. Finally, in the fourth week, Carina sold the last kitten.

Sales situation 2

Right before Carina opened her new shop, she placed a large order for baby rabbits, since Easter was just five weeks away. Carina was pleased to see her weekly sales of the rabbits increase at a constant rate right up until Easter. Immediately afterward, her sales of rabbits dropped sharply before rising much more slowly to the 8-week mark.

Sales situation 3

As Carina was getting ready to open her shop, she wasn't sure how big a market she would have for garden snakes, but she decided to stock them anyway. At the end of eight weeks, her records showed that she had sold the same number of garden snakes each week.

a. Graph 1 matches sales situation _____. Why?

b. Graph 2 matches sales situation _____. Why?

c. Graph 3 matches sales situation _____. Why?

Cutting and Making Solids

Name _____

Below are drawings of six pairs of three-dimensional shapes. For each pair, could you make a single "flat" cut through shape 1 to give you two solids that you could put together to make shape 2? (A "flat" cut slices all the way through the shape, with no curves or angles.)

- Below each pair of shapes, write a description of the cut that you would make.
- Draw line segments on shape 1 to show your cut.
- Mark shape 2 to show your two pieces of shape 1 composed as shape 2.
- Check your answers by working with geoblocks or the electronic 3-D Shape Decomposition Tool, as your teacher directs.

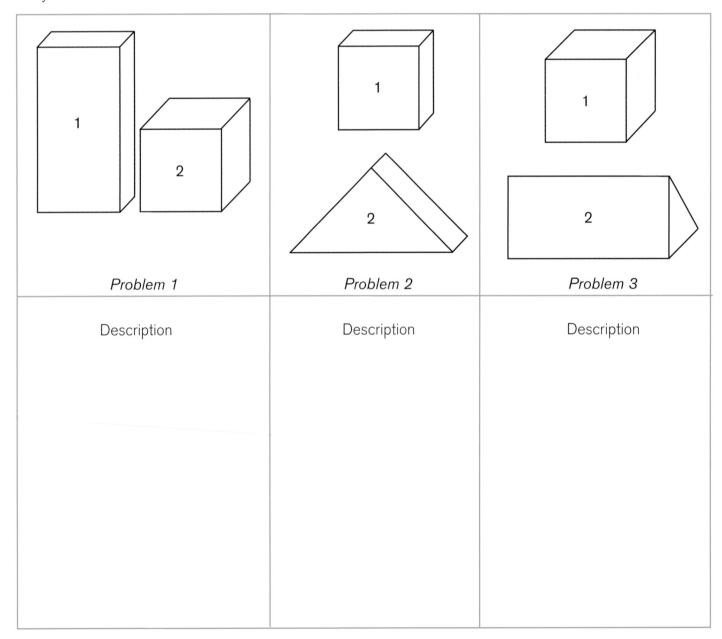

Problem 1	Problem 2	Problem 3
Description	Description	Description

Navigating through Problem Solving and Reasoning in Grade 5

Cutting and Making Solids (continued)

Name _____

Problem 4	*Problem 5*	*Problem 6*
Description	Description	Description

Note: Some of the shapes may not look "right," because the proportions are not what you might expect in drawings of three-dimensional objects. Instead, these drawings preserve lengths, areas, and angles in all "face-on," "top," or "side" views of the shapes. As a result, you can always cut shape 1 into two solids that you can imagine putting together to make shape 2 *exactly as it is drawn on the page.*

Geoblock Comparisons

Name _____

Pictured above are thirteen geoblocks. Problems 1–8 below name particular pairs of these blocks. For each pair, circle the name of the block that you think has the greater volume. If you think that the volumes of the blocks are equal, write "same" beside the pair.

Consider your answers "predictions," which you must then check by working with actual geoblocks. Be prepared to explain why each of your answers is correct.

1. Block A   Block B   _____
2. Block A   Block F   _____
3. Block D   Block G   _____
4. Block B   Block F   _____

5. Block B   Block I   _____
6. Block B   Block K   _____
7. Block D   Block H   _____
8. Block A   Block C   _____

All the blocks have been carefully drawn to preserve lengths, areas, and angles in all "face-on," "top," or "side" views of the shapes. As a result, direct comparisons are possible and fairly easy to make.

Navigating through Problem Solving and Reasoning in Grade 5

Cutting a Rectangular Prism into Congruent Pieces

Name _____

1. *a.* Draw line segments on faces of the rectangular prism below to show a "flat" cut that you could make to slice the prism into two congruent parts. (A "flat" cut slices all the way through the shape, with no curves or angles.) Your cut must pass through edges of the prism at the dots. Use a colored pencil to shade your slicing cut.

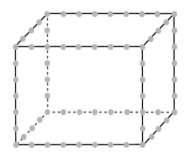

b. See how many more ways you can find to slice the rectangular prism as indicated in 1(*a*).

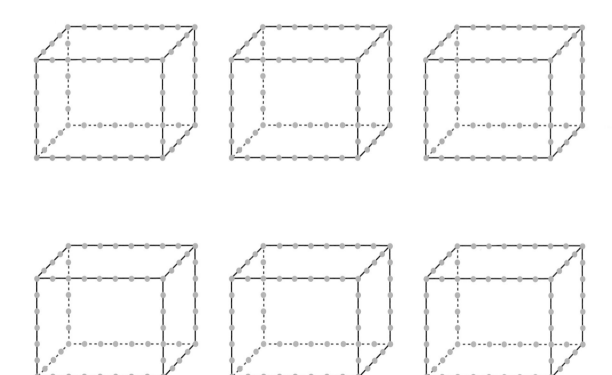

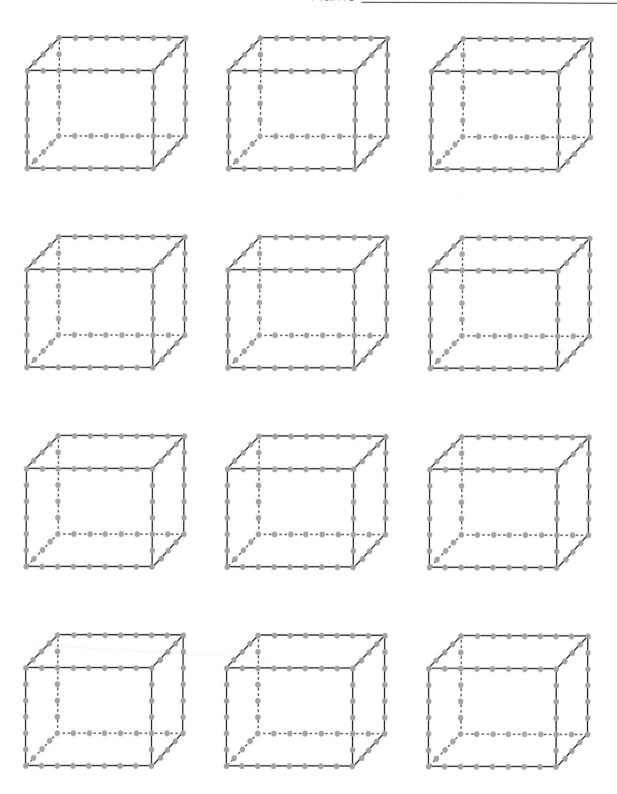

c. Check your answers by using the electronic 3-D Shape Decomposition Tool as your teacher
directs to help you with your work and verify your results.

Name _____

2. *a.* Draw line segments on faces of the rectangular prism below to show *two* flat cuts that you could make to slice the prism into three or four congruent parts. Your cuts must pass through edges of the prism at the dots. Use colored pencils (two different colors) to shade your slicing cuts.

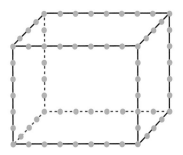

   b. See how many more ways you can find to slice the rectangular prism as indicated in 2(*a*).

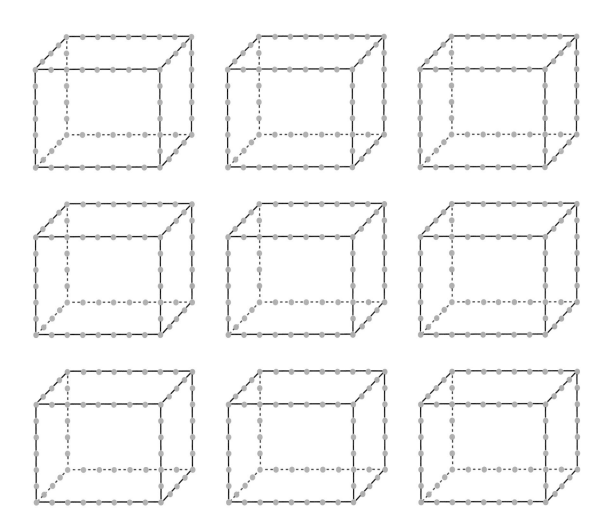

Name _____

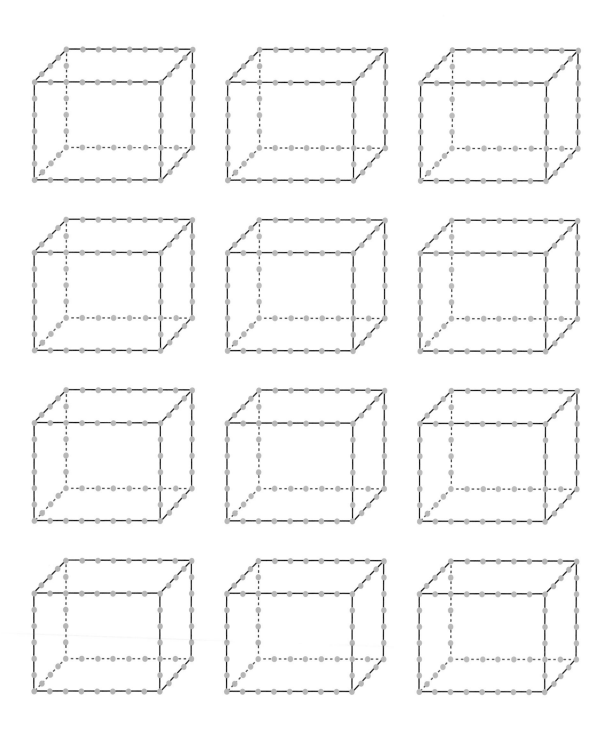

c. Check your answers by using the electronic 3-D Shape Decomposition Tool as your teacher directs to help you with your work and verify your results.

Cross Sections of a Cube

Name _____

A "flat" cut slices all the way through a shape. The flat cut below (shaded) has sliced the cube into two parts.

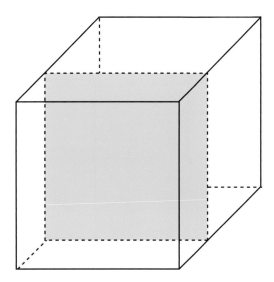

A flat cut exposes a *cross section* of a solid. The cross section is a two-dimensional shape—a *polygon*—whose sides are on faces or edges of a three-dimensional shape and whose area is inside the solid. The cross section made by the flat cut shown above is a square.

Below is a list of some two-dimensional shapes:

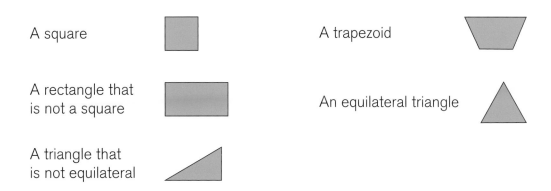

Can you show flat cuts that slice the five cubes on the next page in such a way that you make each two-dimensional shape on the list as a cross section of one of the cubes? *Your cuts must pass through edges of the cube at the dots.* (You should find a cross section that makes a different square from the square shown in the cube above.) Use the 3-D Shape Decomposition Tool as your teacher directs to help you with your work and to verify your results.

Name _____

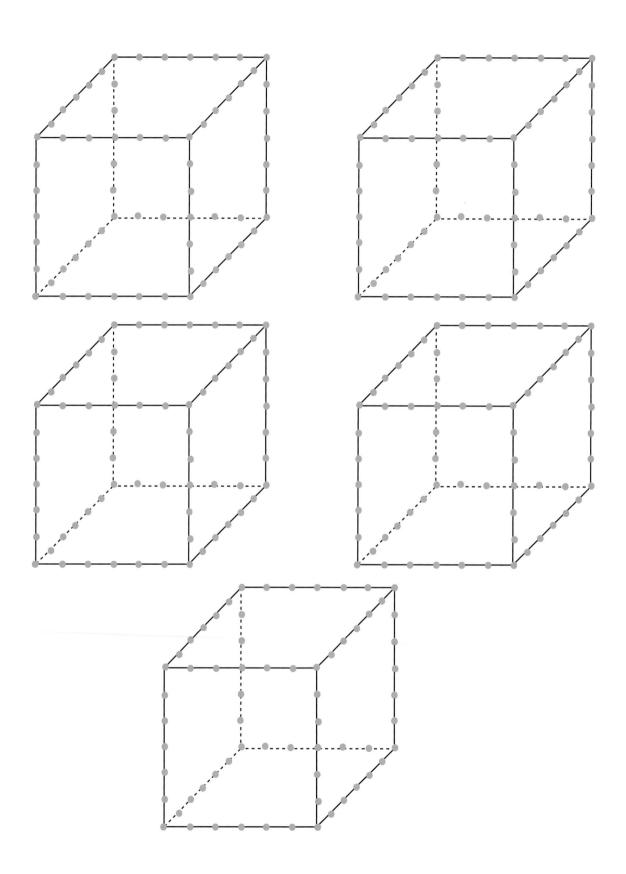

Measuring Up with Animals

Name _____

Do you know who is the fastest runner, the fastest swimmer, the best long jumper, the best pole vaulter, or the strongest weight lifter in the world? If you wanted to identify these *record holders*, you could check in books where records are kept or search on the Internet.

Animals, in a sense, hold records, too. You may read about the fastest animal or the largest animal, for example. When you learn about an animal that holds one of these records, do you ever say to yourself, "Just think how much bigger, or faster, that animal is than I am"?

In the book *Biggest, Strongest, Fastest* (Houghton Mifflin 1995), author Steve Jenkins identifies fourteen different animals that hold world records. The following problems offer opportunities to compare yourself with some of these.

1. The African elephant holds the world record for the heaviest land animal, averaging 22,000 pounds and eating about 300 pounds of grass a day! In the United States, an average 10-year-old boy weighs 85 pounds, and an average 10-year-old girl weighs 88 pounds.[1] Use one of these average weights, or weigh yourself and use your weight in pounds, to answer questions (*a*)–(*e*) below.

    a. How many average 10-year-olds (boys or girls) — or fifth graders whose weight is the same as yours — would it take to equal the record weight of an African elephant?

    b. Do you think the number of children that you found in 1(*a*) would fit (with each child standing on the floor) in an area as large as your classroom? Explain your answer.

    c. Each day, the weight of the grass that an African elephant eats is equivalent to how many times the weight of an average 10-year-old boy or girl — or your weight?

    d. About what fraction of its body weight does the African elephant eat in grass each day?

[1] "Americans Slightly Taller, Much Heavier than 40 Years Ago" (press release, 27 October 2004), National Center for Health Statistics, Center for Disease Control (http://www.cdc.gov/od/oc/media/pressrel/ r041027.htm).

Name _____

e. Suppose that each day a fifth grader needs to eat vegetables that weigh this fraction of his or her body weight. About how many pounds of vegetables would the fifth grader need to eat each day? (Use the weight of an average 10-year-old boy or girl or your own weight.)

2. The giraffe is the world's tallest land animal. A male giraffe can grow to be 19 feet tall! An average 10-year-old boy in the United States is 55.7 inches tall, and an average 10-year-old girl is 56.4 inches.[2]

 a. About how many average 10-year-olds (boys or girls) — or fifth graders whose height is the same as yours — would you need to stack one on top of another to equal the record height of a giraffe?

 b. Suppose you drew a one-inch picture of yourself or an average 10-year-old boy or girl standing straight and tall. How tall would you need to make a giraffe in the same picture to show the proper relationship of heights in the drawing?

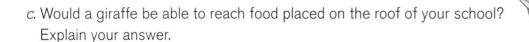

 c. Would a giraffe be able to reach food placed on the roof of your school? Explain your answer.

3. The bird spider, a subspecies of tarantula, lives in South America. Among all the spiders in the world, it holds the record as the largest. Although the bird spider's body measures only about 3 inches in length, it has a leg span of just over 11 inches.

 a. Your teacher has displayed a circle with a diameter of 11 inches on one-inch grid paper. Count squares in the grid to estimate the area occupied by a bird spider with its legs fully extended.

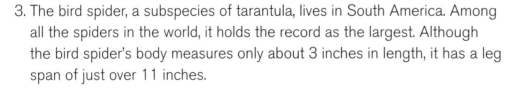

[2]Statistics from the press release from the Center for Disease Control cited in footnote 1.

Name _____

b. Press a hand, with the fingers closed up to one another and the thumb against the hand, on a sheet of one-inch grid paper. Trace around your hand, just up to your wrist. Lift your hand off the paper, and draw a line segment to close the shape on the page. The area of this shape is the area that your hand occupies, just as your teacher's circle shows the area that a bird spider occupies. Count squares in the grid to estimate the area occupied by your hand.

c. How does the area occupied by your hand compare with the area occupied by a bird spider? Compare the two areas by saying how many "hand-areas" you would need to equal the area occupied by the bird spider. (In other words, *Area of my hand* $\times \square = $ *Area of the bird spider.*) Explain your answer.

4. Find another animal (or other phenomenon, such as a mountain) that holds a record. (You can look in a book or on the Internet.)

a. Compare yourself in size or skill with this animal (or other phenomenon). Make your comparison by saying *how many times* larger (or smaller) or more (or less) skillful (or whatever) your animal is than you are.

b. Explain how you made your comparison in (*a*).

Inch Grid Paper

Navigating through Problem Solving and Reasoning in Grade 5

A Snail's Pace

Name _____

The land snail is a very slow animal. In *Biggest, Strongest, Fastest* (Houghton Mifflin 1995), author Steve Jenkins says that the land snail travels only about 8 inches in 1 minute. Have you ever heard someone complain, "We're moving at a snail's pace"? Complete steps 1–6 to compare a snail's pace with your own.

1. Measure your desk from the left edge to the right edge. _____ in.

2. At the rate of 8 inches a minute, how long would it take a land snail to cross your desk?

   _____ min. (Show your work.)

3. Measure the distance in feet from your classroom to the school cafeteria or another location that your teacher selects.

   Location _____

   Distance from the classroom _____ ft.

4. Walk this distance at your usual pace. Use a stopwatch or a wristwatch with a second hand to time yourself. How long did you take? _____ min.

5. How long would it take the snail to travel the same distance? _____ min.
   (Explain how you got your answer.)

6. How many times faster than the snail were you? (Explain how you got your answer.)

Time to Walk vs. Time to Jog

Name _____

How fast do you walk? How fast do you jog? Work in a small group to compile data on the group members' times to walk or jog certain distances. You will do some of the work on the playground or the physical education area, some in the classroom, and some at home, with help from someone in your household.

1. **Go with your group to the playground or physical education area**, depending on your teacher's directions. Your group should bring—

   * one or two yardsticks or measuring tapes
   * a stopwatch or a wristwatch with a second hand
   * one or two pencils
   * a single copy of this activity sheet
   * a copy of the activity sheet "Walking and Jogging Times"
   * a clipboard or a notebook or something similar to press on as you write

2. Work together to estimate a distance of 100 feet over level terrain. Check your group's estimate by measuring the distance and adjusting it to mark out 100 feet.

3. Set up the activity sheet "Walking and Jogging Times" by recording each group member's name in column 1 of the table.

4. Time each group member as he or she walks your measured 100-foot course at a normal, steady pace. Record each time in column 2.

5. Time each group member as he or she jogs this distance at a steady pace. (Group members should not try to run as fast as possible but just jog at a pace that they can maintain.) Record each group member's time in column 3.

6. **Return to the classroom.** Let each group member use his or her own time from step 4 to calculate his or her approximate time to walk one mile. Enter each time in column 4.

7. Let each group member use his or her own time from step 5 to calculate his or her approximate time to jog one mile. Enter the time in column 5.

8. **At home,** ask someone in your household to help you determine the distance to school.

   Distance from my home to school _____ mi.

9. **Back at school,** report this distance to your group, and enter it in column 6 in the table.

10. Use your answers to steps 6 and 7 to find the time it would take you to walk from home to school and the time it would take you to jog from home to school.

11. Discuss your completed table before turning it in to your teacher.

Navigating through Problem Solving and Reasoning in Grade 5

Walking and Jogging Times

Name	Time to walk 100 feet (min.)	Time to jog 100 feet (min.)	Approximate time to walk 1 mile (min.)	Approximate time to jog 1 mile (min.)	Distance from home to school (mi.)	Time to walk from home to school (min.)	Time to jog from home to school (min.)

Faster than a Speeding Ostrich?

Name _____

How far is it from your city to a favorite place that you would like to visit with your class (a nearby beach, national park, or well-known theme park, for example)? How long would it take you to get there? What if you jogged all the way at a steady pace? How about if you flew in a plane? Could a fast animal travel there more quickly than you? Take the following steps to explore such questions.

1. Name a favorite place (in your own region of the country but not in your own city), which you would like to visit with your class.

   My place _____

2. Use a map to figure out how far your place is from your city (for example, the distance from Tampa, Florida, to Orlando, the home of Disney World, is about 90 miles). Record the distance below.

   Distance to my place _____ mi.

3. In the book *What's Faster than a Speeding Cheetah?* (Albert Whitman & Company 1997), author Robert E. Wells gives the speeds of several different animals and motorized vehicles. Some of these appear in the table below.

Animal or Motorized Vehicle	Speed (miles per hour)	Time Needed to Travel to My Place (hours)
You		
Ostrich	45	
Cheetah	70	
Peregrine falcon	200	
Small plane	300	
Jet plane	600	

Note that to fill in the cell for row 2, column 2, you need your speed in miles per hour. In the table ("Walking and Jogging Times") that you completed in "Time to Walk vs. Time to Jog," find the time that you calculated for yourself for jogging a mile. Record that time here.

My estimated time to jog 1 mile _____ min.

Name _____

4. Use your approximate time to jog one mile to find an approximation of the number of miles that you would jog in an hour. This calculation will give you your jogging speed in miles per hour. (Remember that in your calculations you are assuming that you can jog at a steady pace for an indefinite period of time, and this isn't really true.) Enter your speed in row 2, column 2, in the table shown in step 3.

5. Use the distance that you found in step 2 along with the speeds in column 2 in the table in step 3, to compute the times for you, an ostrich, a cheetah, a peregrine falcon, a small plane, and a jet to travel from your city to the favorite place that you identified in step 1.

6. Are you faster than a speeding ostrich?

Is There a Giant in the House?

Name _____

Suppose that a giant has come to live in a gigantic house on your street. Imagine that this giant is 9 feet tall. Also imagine that the giant's proportions — that is, the relationships among the sizes of all the different parts of the giant's body — are exactly the same as yours. However, the giant is "built" on a much larger scale — a gigantic scale, of course!

How would your attributes compare with the giant's?

1. Get ready to make your comparisons by measuring some of your own attributes. (Let a classmate help you, and write the measurements below.)

    a. Your height _____

    b. The length of your arm (from your armpit to the tip of your longest finger) _____

    c. The length of your little finger _____

    d. The length of your foot _____

    e. The width of your foot _____

2. Use the following steps to explore some of the relationships among the measurements of these attributes:

    a. Compare your height with the length of your arm by saying how many arm lengths would equal your height. *Hint*: Your height is how many times the length of your arm? How did you find your answer?

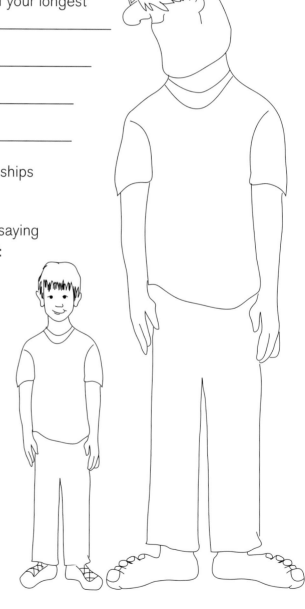

    b. Compare your height with the length of your little finger by saying how many finger lengths would equal your height. How did you find your answer?

Navigating through Problem Solving and Reasoning in Grade 5

Is There a Giant in the House? (continued)

Name _____

c. Compare your height with the length of your foot by saying how many foot lengths would equal your height. How did you find your answer?

d. Compare your height with the width of your foot by saying how many foot widths would equal your height. How did you find your answer?

3. The giant's body has the same proportions as yours. This means that the height of the giant and the giant's arm length compare with each other *in the same way* that your height and your arm length compare with each other. Likewise, the height of the giant compares with the length of the giant's little finger *in the same way* that your height compares with the length of your little finger.

   a. Remember that the giant is 9 feet, or 108 inches, tall. Look back at the measurement you recorded for your own height in 1(*a*). Compare your height with the giant's height by saying how many times taller the giant is than you are. *Hint:* What should go in the box in the equation *My height* × □ = 9 ft?

   b. Use your work in 3(*a*) to help you find approximate sizes for the following parts of the giant's body:

   • The length of the giant's arm _____

   • The length of the giant's little finger _____

   • The length of the giant's foot _____

   • The width of the giant's foot _____

4. How big would the giant's footprint be? Use the following process to find out:

   a. Trace the outline of your foot on a sheet of grid paper from your teacher.

   b. Count squares in the grid to estimate the area of your footprint. Write the approximate area below.

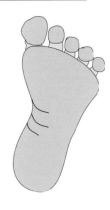

Name _____

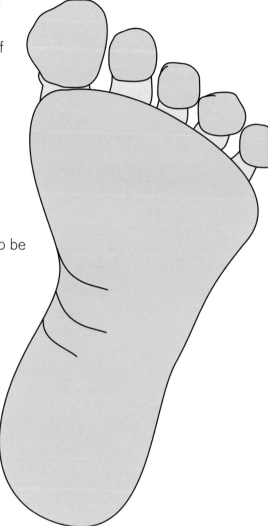

c. The giant's footprint won't fit on a single sheet of grid paper! Your teacher has given you two sheets of grid paper that you can trim and tape together to make space for the giant's big footprint. Use your measurements of the length and width of the giant's foot from problem 3 to sketch an outline of the giant's footprint on grid paper.

d. Count squares in the grid to estimate the area of the giant's footprint. Write the approximate area below.

e. Compare the giant's footprint with your own by saying how many times larger the area of the giant's footprint appears to be than the area of your footprint.

5. Consider an implement that you use every day (like a comb, a toothbrush, a fork, or a pencil).

My item _____

How big would this item need to be for the giant?

a. Draw a sketch of your item in the space below and give its measurements.

Name _____

b. Look back at your work in 3(*a*), where you compared your height and the giant's. Use your work there, along with the measurements in your drawing in 5(*a*), to figure out the measurements of the object for the giant. In the space below (or on another sheet of paper), sketch the object again, this time specifying its giant-sized measurements.

c. Find the dimensions of another object that you use daily. Make a sketch or a model of the giant's version of this object.

Skiing for the First Time?

Skiing can provide some of the greatest thrills in the world of sports. There is nothing like the sensation of soaring down a mountain with plenty of fresh snow or the pleasure of racing your friends to the bottom, meeting new friends on the ski lift, or taking a slower run through the winding trails in the trees.

However, the prospect of skiing can be scary if you've never skied before or haven't skied in a very long time. Skiing may seem even more overwhelming when you hear about all the different types of ski equipment. Knowing about some of the essential gear for skiing can give you a better idea about skiing and simplify your preparations for a skiing trip.

Your first decision will be whether to rent or buy your gear for skiing. You must have the basics: skis, boots, and poles. Beginners often rent their gear so that they can see if they like the sport. Renting also gives first-time skiers an opportunity to become acquainted with the different kinds of equipment before deciding what to buy. Skiers can usually rent equipment from a local ski shop by the day or week.

The next thing that a skier needs to know is that not all skis are the same. When you rent skis, you will have to a make a choice about what type of skis you want. The newest skis, known as "shaped skis," are narrow in the middle and wider at the ends. They make it easier for skiers to turn and stop. "Fat skis" are another type of skis. These skis are designed for handling powdery or chopped-up snow. Fat skis tend to be wider throughout the entire length of the ski.

"Shaped skis" and ski boots
Photo by Michelle Chamberlin

Once you've decided on your skis, you will be ready to pick out your boots. Whether you rent or purchase ski boots, you should always wear them with a pair of socks of medium thickness. The boots should fit snugly on your feet with the socks. Your heel should remain in place when you bend your knee forward, and your toes should barely touch the front edge of the inside of the boot.

Finally, you'll need to pick out your poles. When you bend your arm at the elbow and place the pole in your hand, the pole should just touch the ground.

After you have picked out your skis, boots, and poles, you'll be almost ready to go skiing! In addition to your basic ski gear, you should also have a helmet and goggles for safety on the slopes. Be sure to pack all the items on the list below for your trip.

If you are skiing for the first time, a lesson from a qualified ski instructor can give you a useful introduction to skiing and help you build confidence as a skier. Most ski resorts provide lessons for beginners at reduced rates. Lessons can also be valuable for skiers who are not beginners. Even when you've mastered the basics of skiing and have skied for several days, consider taking lessons from time to time to continue improving your skiing skills.

Nakiska Ski Resort in the Canadian Rockies
Photo by Scott Chamberlin

Items to Pack for a One-Day Ski Trip
Don't forget these essentials when you pack!

• Long underwear	• Turtleneck	• Sweater	• Ski jacket and ski pants
• Lightweight parka	• Hat and goggles	• Neck warmer	• Gloves or mittens
• Helmet	• Headband	• Sunglasses	• Sunscreen
• Socks	• Money	• Phone numbers	• Skis, boots, and poles
• Heat Packs	• Camera		

What Do You Know about It Now?

Name _____

What have you learned about skiing by reading about it? Answer the following questions to show what you now know.

1. What basic equipment will you need if you decide to go skiing?

2. There are many different types of skis. Can you name two types?

3. How can you tell if your boots fit correctly for skiing?

4. Skiing is particularly enjoyable right after new snow has fallen. The more snow, the better! Examine the following data on snow at three local ski resorts.

New Snow Today (in Inches)		
Spring Valley Ski Resort	Big Mountain Ski Resort	Sky High Ski Resort
2.5	5.0	3.2

Which resort would be your first choice for a ski trip?

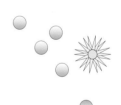

Which would be your third choice?

Name _____

5. Using the data in the table below, can you give the snowfall for February 5, 2005, at White Hills Ski Resort?

Daily Snowfall (in Inches) at White Hills Ski Resort
January–April, 2004–2005

Day	January 2004	January 2005	February 2004	February 2005	March 2004	March 2005	April 2004	April 2005
1	2	0	3	0	0	3	1	0
2	0	0	1	1	7	2	2	2
3	0	1	4	3	8	1	1	0
4	0	3	5	4	3	3	2	0
5	4	4	0	7	4	9	2	0
6	0	5	0	1	0	0	0	4

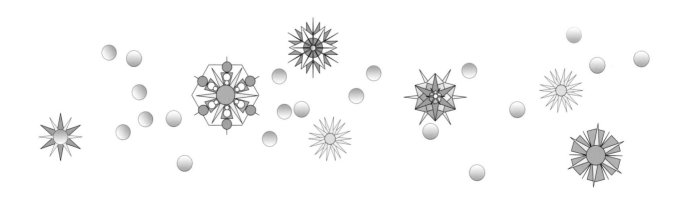

Which Month to Ski?

Name _____

Last summer, as a community service project, the Brown County Youth Club helped clean the roadsides along Highway 68, which leads to White Hills Ski Resort. To thank the youth group for its work, the resort has invited members of the group to come and ski, free of charge, on a Saturday of their choosing in the next January, February, March, or April. The group wants to narrow down its decision to the month that is likely to have the most snow. Thus, the group has asked White Hills Ski Resort for information about its daily snowfall during these months in past years. The club received the following table of information from the resort for the ski months in the years 2004 and 2005.

Daily Snowfall (in Inches) at White Hills Ski Resort
January–April, 2004–2005

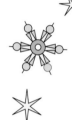

Day	January 2004	January 2005	February 2004	February 2005	March 2004	March 2005	April 2004	April 2005
1	2	0	3	0	0	3	1	0
2	0	0	1	1	7	2	2	2
3	0	1	4	3	8	1	1	0
4	0	3	5	4	3	3	2	0
5	4	4	0	7	4	9	2	0
6	0	5	0	1	0	0	0	4
7	1	0	4	0	0	0	1	5
8	1	1	3	0	1	5	3	4
9	0	0	4	0	5	6	1	3
10	0	2	5	0	4	1	2	2
11	5	3	0	8	2	2	3	2
12	1	0	0	4	3	1	2	0
13	4	0	10	5	8	4	0	3
14	0	0	1	0	0	0	0	2
15	0	1	2	1	3	2	2	3
16	0	0	0	5	2	0	0	4
17	1	0	2	2	1	2	2	0
18	0	0	4	3	1	0	0	4
19	3	4	6	0	0	1	2	0
20	0	2	0	1	0	0	3	2

Name _____

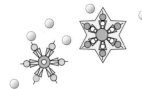

Daily Snowfall (in Inches) at White Hills Ski Resort
January–April, 2004–2005 (continued)

Day	January 2004	January 2005	February 2004	February 2005	March 2004	March 2005	April 2004	April 2005
21	2	0	0	6	0	0	1	2
22	3	4	1	4	0	1	0	1
23	0	3	2	4	2	5	0	2
24	0	0	1	1	5	0	1	0
25	1	1	6	0	3	1	2	6
26	1	0	4	0	4	4	5	0
27	0	0	4	3	8	0	2	1
28	3	0	0	0	2	0	0	2
29	5	1	0	–––	0	0	1	1
30	0	1	–––	–––	4	3	0	0
31	0	2	–––	–––	1	1	–––	–––

The Brown County Youth Club needs your help in deciding which month to choose for its skiing trip. Scheduling difficulties may rule out Saturdays in the group's first-choice month, so the club is asking you to rank the four months from "best" to "worst" — that is, from most likely to least likely to offer good snow for skiing. Write a letter to the Brown County Youth Club with your rankings, and explain how you made your decisions.

Also, the youth group might decide to make this ski trip an annual event. If so, the members might want to use your method to reconsider their choice of the best month to ski in future years, when they would have additional daily snowfall data to analyze. As a result, the club would like a step-by-step description of your method for making a decision and ranking the months.

Another Year of Snow

Name _____

Below is a table that shows daily snowfall, in inches, at White Hills Ski Resort for the months of January–April in three consecutive years, 2004–2006. Thus, the table shows the daily snowfall data that you analyzed in "Best Month to Ski," plus new data on daily snowfall for January–April in the next year, 2006. Do the new data in this extended data set change your rankings of the months January–April from "best month to ski" (1) to "worst month to ski" (4)?

Daily Snowfall (in Inches) at White Hills Ski Resort
January–April, 2004–2006

Day	January 2004	January 2005	January 2006	February 2004	February 2005	February 2006	March 2004	March 2005	March 2006	April 2004	April 2005	April 2006
1	2	0	2	3	0	7	0	3	0	1	0	1
2	0	0	1	1	1	5	7	2	0	2	2	2
3	0	1	0	4	3	2	8	1	3	1	0	1
4	0	3	0	5	4	0	3	3	5	2	0	0
5	4	4	0	0	7	3	4	9	0	2	0	2
6	0	5	2	0	1	0	0	0	2	0	4	2
7	1	0	0	4	0	0	0	0	4	1	5	4
8	1	1	0	3	0	3	1	5	5	3	4	5
9	0	0	1	4	0	5	5	6	0	1	3	2
10	0	2	5	5	0	6	4	1	0	2	2	1
11	5	3	0	0	8	2	2	2	6	3	2	2
12	1	0	6	0	4	0	3	1	1	2	0	0
13	4	0	7	10	5	0	8	4	2	0	3	0
14	0	0	2	1	0	1	0	0	1	0	2	3
15	0	1	3	2	1	0	3	2	1	2	3	1
16	0	0	0	0	5	2	2	0	0	0	4	2
17	1	0	0	2	2	7	1	2	1	2	0	3
18	0	0	5	4	3	0	1	0	0	0	4	2
19	3	4	0	6	0	5	0	1	3	2	0	3
20	0	2	0	0	1	4	0	0	8	3	2	2
21	2	0	1	0	6	5	0	0	6	1	2	1

Name _____

Daily Snowfall (in Inches) at White Hills Ski Resort
January–April, 2004–2006 (continued)

Day	January 2004	January 2005	January 2006	February 2004	February 2005	February 2006	March 2004	March 2005	March 2006	April 2004	April 2005	April 2006
22	3	4	2	1	4	0	0	1	2	0	1	0
23	0	3	0	2	4	7	2	5	0	0	2	4
24	0	0	2	1	1	8	5	0	7	1	0	5
25	1	1	0	6	0	3	3	1	7	2	6	1
26	1	0	0	4	0	0	4	4	6	5	0	1
27	0	0	2	4	3	0	8	0	2	2	1	2
28	3	0	0	0	0	2	2	0	1	0	2	1
29	5	1	0	0	–––	–––	0	0	3	1	1	0
30	0	1	0	–––	–––	–––	4	3	4	0	0	1
31	0	2	1	–––	–––	–––	1	1	2	–––	–––	–––

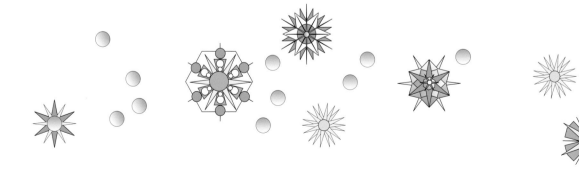

Solutions for "Can You Divide It Evenly?"

Number \ Divided by	2?	3?	4?	5?	6?	8?	9?	10?
1								
2	Y							
3		Y						
4	Y		Y					
5				Y				
6	Y	Y			Y			
7								
8	Y		Y			Y		
9		Y					Y	
10	Y			Y				Y
11								
12	Y	Y	Y		Y			
13								
14	Y							
15		Y		Y				
16	Y		Y			Y		
17								
18	Y	Y			Y		Y	
19								
20	Y		Y	Y				Y
21		Y						
22	Y							
23								
24	Y	Y	Y		Y	Y		
25				Y				
26	Y							
27		Y					Y	
28	Y		Y					
29								
30	Y	Y		Y	Y			Y
31								
32	Y		Y			Y		
33		Y						
34	Y							
35				Y				
36	Y	Y	Y		Y		Y	
37								
38	Y							
39		Y						
40	Y		Y	Y		Y		Y

Number	2?	3?	4?	5?	6?	8?	9?	10?
41								
42	Y	Y			Y			
43								
44	Y		Y					
45		Y		Y			Y	
46	Y							
47								
48	Y	Y	Y		Y	Y		
49								
50	Y			Y				Y
51		Y						
52	Y		Y					
53								
54	Y	Y			Y		Y	
55				Y				
56	Y		Y			Y		
57		Y						
58	Y							
59								
60	Y	Y	Y	Y	Y			Y
61								
62	Y							
63		Y					Y	
64	Y		Y			Y		
65				Y				
66	Y	Y			Y			
67								
68	Y		Y					
69		Y						
70	Y			Y				Y
71								
72	Y	Y	Y		Y	Y	Y	
73								
74	Y							
75		Y		Y				
76	Y		Y					
77								
78	Y	Y			Y			
79								
80	Y		Y	Y		Y		Y
81		Y					Y	
82	Y							
83								
84	Y	Y	Y		Y			
85				Y				

Solutions for "Can You Divide It Evenly?"(continued)

Number \ Divided by	2?	3?	4?	5?	6?	8?	9?	10?
86	Y							
87		Y						
88	Y		Y			Y		
89								
90	Y	Y		Y	Y		Y	Y
91								
92	Y		Y					
93		Y						
94	Y							
95				Y				
96	Y	Y	Y		Y	Y		
97								
98	Y							
99		Y					Y	
100	Y		Y	Y				Y

Solutions for "How Do You Know It's Divisible?"

Figure 1 in the text shows the characteristics of numbers that are divisible by 2–10 (excluding 7).

Solutions for "A PIN for Mr. Mitchell"

The PINs that your students create for Mr. Mitchell may vary since seven combinations of the digits will satisfy Mr. Mitchell's conditions. The possibilities are identified and discussed in the text (see pp. 14–15).

Solutions for "Projecting from Patterns"

Week	Guinea Pig Sales
1	2
2	4
3	6
4	8
5	10
6	12
7	14
8	16
n	$2n$

Week	Gerbil Sales
1	6
2	12
3	18
4	24
5	30
6	36
7	42
8	48
n	$6n$

Week	Hamster Sales
1	3
2	6
3	9
4	12
5	15
6	18
7	21
8	24
n	$3n$

Corresponding graphs appear in figures 5, 6, and 7, and are discussed in the text.

Solutions for "Animal Accounting"

1. The students use *n* to stand for the number of weeks that Carina's pet shop has been in business.
   a. The number of guinea pig sales each week is equal to $2n$.
   b. The number of gerbil sales each week is equal to $6n$.
   c. The number of hamster sales each week is equal to $3n$.

2. *a* and *b.* If the rate remained constant through week 20, Carina would sell 36 guinea pigs in week 18
   ($n = 18$; $2n = 2 \times 18 = 36$).

   c and *d.* If the rate remained constant through week 20, Carina would sell 120 gerbils in week 20;
   ($n = 20$; $6n = 6 \times 20 = 120$).

3. Graph 1 matches sales situation 3. Graph 2 matches sales situation 1. Graph 3 matches sales situation 2. Solutions are discussed in the text (see pp. 29–30.)

Solutions for "Cutting and Making Solids"

Students' descriptions will vary. For each pair of shapes, a cut to decompose shape 1 into two parts that can be recomposed the parts as shape 2 is shown below. Segments in blue on shape 1 show the cut; segments in blue on shape 2 show the joining of the two parts to compose shape 2.

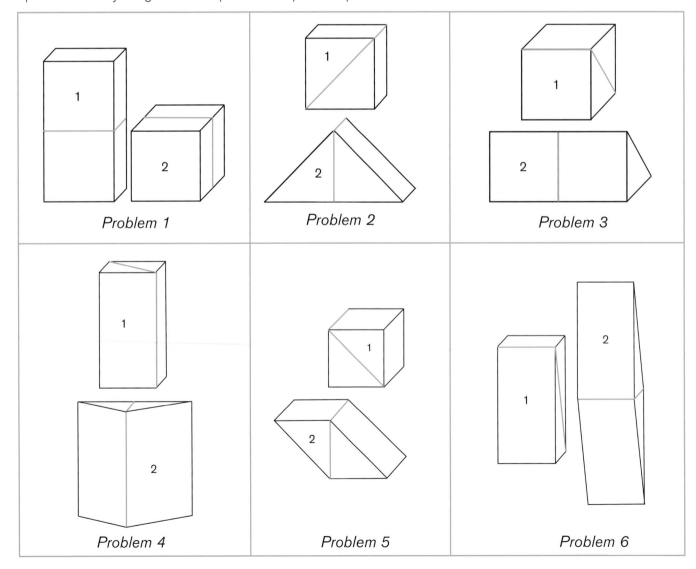

Problem 1 *Problem 2* *Problem 3*

Problem 4 *Problem 5* *Problem 6*

Navigating through Problem Solving and Reasoning in Grade 5

Solutions for "Geoblock Comparisons"

1. Block A has a greater volume than block B. (The volume of block A is twice that of block B.)
2. Block A has a greater volume than block F. (The volume of block A is twice that of block F.)
3. Block D has a greater volume than block G. (The volume of block D is twice that of block G.)
4. The volumes of blocks B and F are the same.
5. The volumes of blocks B and I are the same.
6. The volumes of blocks B and K are the same.
7. The volumes of blocks D and H are the same.
8. The volumes of blocks A and C are the same.

Solutions for "Cutting a Rectangular Prism into Congruent Pieces"

1. *a* and *b*. Below are eighteen unique ways (except for rotations or reflections) to use a single planar cut to slice the pictured prism at dots and produce congruent parts.

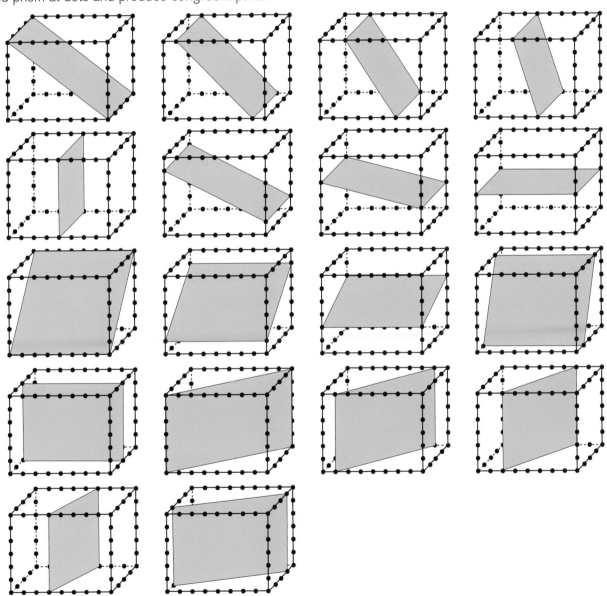

2. *a* and *b*. Figure 18a in the text shows how to use two planar cuts through dots to divide the pictured rectangular prism into three parts. With the restriction that the cuts must pass through dots, this is the only way to use two cuts to produce three congruent parts. Below are eighteen unique ways to use two planar cuts to slice the prism at dots and produce four congruent parts. Note that each of these is a solution from problem 1 with the second cut slicing through the congruent pieces formed by the first cut, to yield four congruent solids.

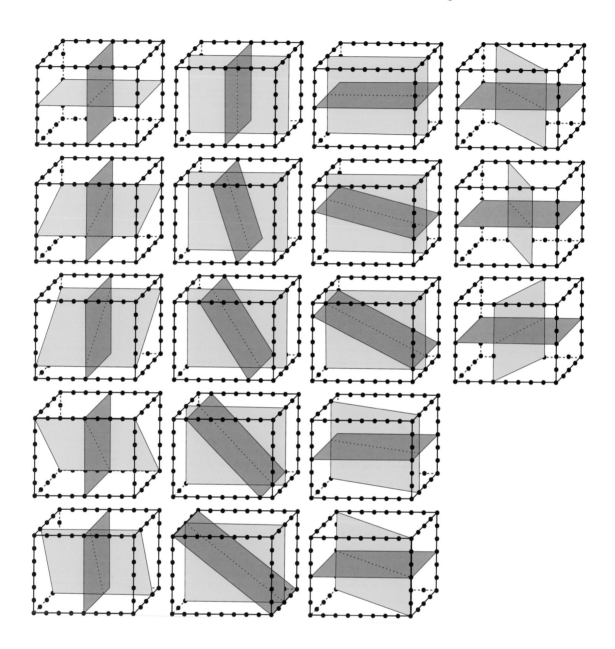

Solutions for "Cross Sections of a Cube"

Students' solutions will vary. There are multiple ways to use a single planar cut to slice the pictured cube at dots and produce cross sections that form the specified polygons. Figure 19 in the text shows sample solutions.

Solutions for "Measuring Up with Animals"

1. Answers will vary. The following sample responses use a weight of 85 pounds — the weight of an average 10-year-old boy in the United States.

   a. It would take approximately 259 students to equal the weight (22,000 pounds) of an African elephant: $22{,}000 \div 85 \approx 259$.

   b. Students' answers will vary. To determine whether 259 students would fit into the classroom, a student could use the following process:

   • "Pack" four students in two tight rows, with the students in each row standing shoulder to shoulder, and the second row standing in front of the first, as close to it as possible.

   • Measure the "breadth" of a student — that is, the distance in a row from a student's left shoulder to the left shoulder of the student beside him, for example.

   • Measure the "thickness " of a student — that is, the distance from the back of one student to the back of the student in front of him, for example.

   • Determine the area of classroom floor that a student would occupy.

   • Measure the dimensions of the classroom and find its area.

   • Divide the area of the classroom by the area occupied by one student. If the quotient is greater than 259, then 259 students could stand shoulder to shoulder and front to back in the classroom. (Or, alternatively, multiply the area occupied by one student by 259. If the product is less than the area of the classroom, then 259 students would fit in the room.)

   c. Each day, the weight of the grass that an African elephant eats is equivalent to three to four times the weight of an average 10-year-old boy: $300 \div 85 \approx 3.53$.

   d. An elephant eats grass that weighs about $\frac{1}{73}$, or approximately 1.4 percent, of its weight each day:

   $$\frac{300}{22000} = \frac{3}{220} \approx 0.014.$$

   So an 85-pound 10-year-old would eat about (85×0.014), or 1.19, pounds of vegetables each day.

2. Answers will vary. The following sample responses use a height of 56.4 inches — the height of an average 10-year-old girl in the United States.

   a. It would take approximately four 10-year-old girls, stacked head to foot, to equal the record height of a giraffe (19 ft $\times$ 12 in = 228 in): $228 \div 56.4 \approx 4.04$.

   b. If a scale drawing showed a 10-year-old girl and a giraffe and represented the girl's actual height (56.4 inches) as 1 inch, it would show the giraffe's height as approximately 4 inches: $228 \div 56.4 \approx 4.04$.

   c. Answers will vary, depending on the height of the school.

3. a. The area of a circle with a diameter of 11 inches is approximately 95 square inches. The size of the squares in the grid will affect the precision of the students' estimate of the area; the smaller the grid, the more precise the estimate can be. However, it is harder for students to count a large number of very small squares, so inch grid paper is probably the most practical size for this exercise.

   b. Answers will vary as students count squares to estimate the area that their handprint occupies.

   c. Some students may use additive reasoning to find the difference between the two areas. Encourage them to use multiplicative reasoning by thinking of the area occupied by the bird spider as larger than the area occupied by the handprint by a particular factor. Multiplying the area of the handprint by the factor gives the area occupied by the bird spider.

4. Answers will vary. As discussed in the text, one fifth grader compared her height with the reach of a sun jellyfish (see p. 50).

Solutions for "A Snail's Pace"

Answers will vary. As discussed in the text (see p. 51), some fifth graders completed the activity without actually finding the total distance from their classroom to a second, specified location. Instead, they marked off 8-inch segments in the distance and counted the segments. The number of segments is equal to the number of minutes that the snail needed to travel the distance.

Solutions for "Time to Walk vs. Time to Jog"

1 and 2. Be sure that your students estimate a 100-foot course before actually measuring. This exercise will help students improve their ability to estimate larger distances in the future.

3 and 4. Observe your students as they time one another in walking the measured course. Check to be sure that the students are being consistent as they determine the beginning and end of their measurements of time.

5. Students' walking times will generally vary between 19 and 29 seconds (0.32 and 0.48 minutes) for 100 feet. Jogging times will generally vary between 8 and 18 seconds (0.13 and 0.3 minutes).

6. Answers will vary. Guide your students as necessary in estimating their times for walking a mile. The students should know that 1 mile = 5280 feet. There are 52.8 groups of 100 feet in a mile. Each student can multiply his or her time to walk 100 feet by 52.8 to find his or her time to walk one mile.

7. Answers will vary. Students can use the same process as in step 6 to estimate their times for jogging a mile. (Each student can multiply his or her time to jog 100 feet by 52.8 to find his or her time to jog one mile.)

8 and 9. Answers will vary.

10. Once each student has determined the distance from home to school, the student can use his or her estimate of the time to walk or jog one mile to estimate the time that he or she would take to walk or jog the distance from home to school. The student can multiply the time for a mile by the distance (in miles) from home to school to find the walking or jogging time to school.

Solutions for "Faster than a Speeding Ostrich?"

Answers will vary. In the table below, the times in rows 3–7 are based on a distance of 90 miles.

Animal or Vehicle	Speed (miles per hour)	Time Needed (hours)
You		
Ostrich	45	2.00
Cheetah	70	1.30
Peregrine falcon	200	0.45
Small plane	300	0.30
Jet plane	600	0.15

Solutions for "Is There a Giant in the House?"

1. Answers will vary. For many fifth-grade children, heights range from slightly more than 4 feet to around 5 feet. Arm lengths range from about 21 to 30 inches; the length of little fingers is around 2 inches or slightly more.

2. Answers will vary. Be sure that your students use multiplicative reasoning to make these comparisons. Students should divide their height by their arm length, length of little finger, foot length, or foot width to find the required comparisons. The decimal obtained from each division gives a factor that the student can use in establishing measurements for the giant in step 3.

3. For a student who is 53 inches tall with an arm length of 21 inches, the ratio of height to arm length is $\frac{53}{21} = 2.52$.

   Hence, the giant's ratio of height to arm length should also be 2.52. Because the giant is 9 feet, or 108 inches, tall, his arm length is $\frac{108}{2.52}$ inches $= 42.86$ inches ≈ 43 inches.

   Alternatively (and perhaps more simply), the students can compare the one measurement that they know for the giant — a height of 9 feet — with their own height. Because each student is assuming that the giant is proportioned in every respect exactly like himself or herself, the ratio of 9 feet to the student's own height will give a multiplier that the student can use with any of his or her measurements in step 1 to find measurements of corresponding features of the giant. Nine feet equals 108 inches. Using the example above, we can say that the ratio of the giant's height (108 inches) to the height (53 inches) of the student is $\frac{108}{53} \approx 2.04$. Because the giant is proportioned exactly like the student, 2.04 is the multiplier to use with each student-sized measurement to determine each giant-sized counterpart. If the student's arm length is 21 inches, the giant's arm length is about 43 inches: $21 \times 2.04 = 42.86 \approx 43$.

   Thus, we have arrived at the same measurement as before, by a slightly different route — one that may be clearer to the students.

4. Answers will vary. Be sure that your students use multiplicative reasoning rather than additive reasoning to make the comparison between the giant's footprint and their own.

5. Answers will vary. Students can determine measurements for a giant-sized object by using comparisons similar to those in step 3.

Solutions for "Which Month to Ski?"

Students' solutions will vary, and sample solutions from students are presented and discussed in the text and on the CD-ROM.

References

Battista, Michael T. "How Many Blocks?" *Mathematics Teaching in the Middles Grades* 3 (March/April 1998): 404–11.

———. "The Importance of Spatial Structuring in Geometric Reasoning." *Teaching Children Mathematics* 6 (November 1999): 170–77.

———. "The Development of a Cognition-Based Assessment System for Core Mathematics Concepts in Grades K–5." National Science Foundation project, 2001.

———. "Building Properly Structured Mental Models for Reasoning about Volume." *ON-Math: Online Journal of School Mathematics* 1 (Winter 2002), http://my.nctm.org/eresources/journal_home.asp?journal_id=6.

Battista, Michael T., and Mary Berle-Carman. *Containers and Cubes.* Palo Alto, Calif.: Dale Seymour Publications, 1996.

Bennett, Albert B., Jr., and L. Ted Nelson. "Divisibility Tests: So Right for Discoveries." *Mathematics Teaching in the Middle School* 7 (April 2002): 460–64.

DeFrancisco, Carrie, and Marilyn Burns. *Lessons for Decimals and Percents: Grades 5–6.* Teaching Arithmetic. Sausalito, Calif.: Math Solutions, 2002.

Doerr, Helen M., and Lyn D. English. "A Modeling Perspective on Students' Mathematical Reasoning about Data." *Journal for Research in Mathematics Education* 34 (March 2003): 110–36.

Fennema, Elizabeth, Thomas P. Carpenter, Megan L. Franke, Linda Levi, Victoria R. Jacobs, and Susan B. Empson. "A Longitudinal Study of Learning to Use Children's Thinking in Mathematics Instruction." *Journal for Research in Mathematics Education* 27 (July 1996): 403–34.

Fraivillig, Judith. "Strategies for Advancing Children's Mathematical Thinking." *Teaching Children Mathematics* 7 (April 2001): 454–59.

Hendrix-Martin, Eunice. "Students Use Their Bodies to Measure Animals." *Teaching Children Mathematics* 3 (April 1997): 426–30.

Henningsen, Marjorie, and Mary Kay Stein. "Mathematical Tasks and Student Cognition: Classroom-Based Factors That Support and Inhibit High-Level Mathematical Thinking and Reasoning." *Journal for Research in Mathematics Education* 28 (November 1997): 524–49.

National Council of Teachers of Mathematics (NCTM). *Principles and Standards for School Mathematics.* Reston, Va.: NCTM, 2000.

———. *Curriculum Focal Points for Prekindergarten through Grade 8 Mathematics: A Quest for Coherence.* Reston, Va.: NCTM, 2006.

Oleson, Vicki L. "*Incredible Comparisons:* Experiences with Data Collection." *Teaching Children Mathematics* 5 (September 1998): 12–16.

Schroeder, Thomas L., and Frank K. Lester, Jr. "Developing Understanding in Mathematics via Problem Solving." In *New Directions for Elementary School Mathematics,* 1989 Yearbook of the National Council of Teachers of Mathematics, edited by Paul R. Trafton, pp. 31–42. Reston, Va.: National Council of Teachers of Mathematics, 1989.

Smith, Margaret Schwan, and Mary Kay Stein. "Selecting and Creating Mathematical Tasks: From Research to Practice." *Mathematics Teaching in the Middle School* 3 (February 1998): 344–50.

Stein, Mary Kay, Barbara W. Grover, and Marjorie Henningsen. "Building Student Capacity for Mathematical Thinking and Reasoning: An Analysis of Mathematical Tasks Used in Reform Classrooms." *American Educational Research Journal* 33 (1996): 455–88.

Stein, Mary Kay, and Margaret Schwan Smith. "Mathematical Tasks as a Framework for Reflection: From Research to Practice." *Mathematics Teaching in the Middle School* 3 (January 1998): 268–75.

Thompson, Denisse R., Richard A. Austin, and Charlene E. Beckmann. "Using Literature as a Vehicle to Explore Proportional Reasoning." In *Making Sense of Fractions, Ratios, and Proportions*, 2002 Yearbook of the National Council of Teachers of Mathematics (NCTM), edited by Bonnie Litwiller, pp. 130–37. Reston, Va.: NCTM, 2002.

Yeatts, Karol, Michael T. Battista, Sally Mayberry, Denisse R. Thompson, and Judith S. Zawojewski. *Navigating through Problem Solving and Reasoning in Grade 3. Principles and Standards for School Mathematics* Navigations Series. Reston, Va.: National Council of Teachers of Mathematics, 2004.

———. *Navigating through Problem Solving and Reasoning in Grade 4. Principles and Standards for School Mathematics Navigations* Series. Reston, Va.: National Council of Teachers of Mathematics, 2005.

Wickett, Maryann, and Marilyn Burns. *Lessons for Introducing Place Value: Grade 2.* Teaching Arithmetic. Sausalito, Calif.: Math Solutions, 2002.

Wickett, Maryann, Susan Ohanian, and Marilyn Burns. *Introducing Division: Grades 3–4.* Teaching Arithmetic. Sausalito, Calif.: Math Solutions, 2002.

Suggested Reading

Carroll, William M., and Denise Porter. "Alternative Algorithms for Whole-Number Operations." In *The Teaching and Learning of Algorithms in School Mathematics*, 1998 Yearbook of the National Council of Teachers of Mathematics (NCTM), edited by Lorna J. Morrow, pp. 106–14. Reston, Va.: NCTM, 1998.

Crawford, Ann R., and William E. Scott. "Making Sense of Slope." *Mathematics Teacher* 93 (February 2000): 114–18.

Piez, Cynthia M., and Mary H. Voxman. "Multiple Representations—Using Different Perspectives to Form a Clearer Picture." *Mathematics Teacher* 90 (February 1997): 164–66.

Randolph, Tamela D., and Helene J. Sherman. "Alternative Algorithms: Increasing Options, Reducing Errors." *Teaching Children Mathematics* 7 (April 2001): 480–84.

Smith, Margaret Schwan. "Redefining Success in Mathematics Teaching and Learning." *Mathematics Teaching in the Middle School* 5 (February 2000) 378–82; 86.

Wood, Terry, and Tammy Turner-Vorbeck. "Extending the Conception of Mathematics Teaching." In *Beyond Classical Pedagogy: Teaching Elementary School Mathematics*, edited by Terry Wood, Barbara Scott Nelson, and Janet Warfield, pp. 185–208. Mahwah, N.J.: Lawrence Erlbaum Associates, 2001.

Zawojewski, Judith S. "Polishing a Data Task: Seeking Better Assessment." *Teaching Children Mathematics* 2 (February 1996): 372–78.

Zawojewski, Judith S., Richard Lesh, and Lyn D. English. "A Models and Modeling Perspective on the Role of Small Group Learning Activities." In *Beyond Constructivism: Models and Modeling Perspectives on Mathematics Problem Solving, Learning, and Teaching*, edited by Richard Lesh and Helen M. Doerr, pp. 337–58. Mahwah, N.J.: Lawrence Erlbaum Associates, 2003.

Children's Literature

Teachers may wish to incorporate appropriate literature into the investigations in this book. For children's books that are suitable for particular mathematics topics, teachers may refer to *The Wonderful World of Mathematics: A Critically Annotated List of Children's Books in Mathematics*, by Dianne Thiessen, Margaret Matthias, and Jacqueline Smith (Reston, Va: NCTM, 1989). The examples of children's literature that are cited in the text follow:

Ash, Russell. *Incredible Comparisons*. London: Dorling Kindersley, 1996.

Brenner, Barbara. *Wagon Wheels*. New York: Harper and Row, 1978.

Briggs, Raymond. *Jim and the Beanstalk*. New York: Coward-McCann, 1970.

Hodges, Margaret. *Gulliver in Lilliput*. New York: Holiday House, 1995.

Jenkins, Steve. *Biggest, Strongest, Fastest*. New York: Tichnor and Fields, 1995.

Long, Lynette. *Dazzling Division: Games and Activities That Make Math Easy and Fun*. New York: John Wiley and Sons, 2000.

Malam, John. *Highest, Longest, Deepest: A Fold-Out Guide to the World's Record Breakers*. New York: Simon and Schuster, 1996.

Most, Bernard. *How Big Were the Dinosaurs?* San Diego: Harcourt Brace and Company, 1994.

Pinczes, Elinor J. *One Hundred Hungry Ants*. New York: Houghton Mifflin, 1993.

Schwartz, David. *If You Hopped Like a Frog*. New York: Scholastic Press, 1999.

Wells, Robert E. *What's Faster than a Speeding Cheetah?* Morton Grove, Ill.: Albert Whitman and Company, 1997.

Teachers may also wish to refer to the following books:

- *Exploring Mathematics through Literature: Articles and Lessons for Prekindergarten through Grade 8*, edited by Dianne Thiessen (NCTM 2004). This book provides classroom examples of the use of children's literature to teach problem solving, representation, and reasoning.

- *New Visions for Linking Literature and Mathematics*, by David J. Whitin and Phyllis Whitin (NCTM/National Council of Teachers of English 2004). This book helps teachers find and use age-appropriate children's books with mathematical content.